Thomas Harvey Skinner

Discussions in Theology

Thomas Harvey Skinner

Discussions in Theology

ISBN/EAN: 9783743420120

Manufactured in Europe, USA, Canada, Australia, Japa

Cover: Foto ©Lupo / pixelio.de

Manufactured and distributed by brebook publishing software (www.brebook.com)

Thomas Harvey Skinner

Discussions in Theology

DISCUSSIONS

IN THEOLOGY.

BY

THOMAS H. SKINNER,
PROFESSOR IN THE UNION THEOLOGICAL SEMINARY.

NEW YORK:
ANSON D. F. RANDOLPH,
No. 770 BROADWAY.
1868.

Entered according to the Act of Congress in the year 1868,

BY ANSON D. F. RANDOLPH,

in the Clerk's Office of the District Court of the United States, for the Southern District of New York.

EDWARD O. JENKINS,
PRINTER AND STEREOTYPER,
20 North William Street.

PREFACE.

This volume is a Second Edition of the Miscellanies it contains. They have been collected out of Periodicals, in which at different times they were printed. They have been carefully revised, and it is hoped, now appear in a better than their original form. The subjects of them are important, and however imperfectly treated in these small papers, have not been discussed without a deep sense of their value. The author has been induced to prepare the little book which embodies them, by a desire to give whatever of truthfulness and sound teaching may be found in them, more emphasis and more influence than it might otherwise have had.

CONTENTS.

I.—MIRACLES THE PROOF OF CHRISTIANITY, . . 1
II.—NATURE OF THE ATONEMENT, ... 39
III.—NATURE OF THE ATONEMENT—Continued, . . 57
IV.—CHRIST PRE-EXISTENT, ... 73
V.—CHRIST PREACHING TO THE SPIRITS IN PRISON, ... 99
VI.—IMPOTENCE OF WILL: WILL-NOT A REAL CAN-NOT, ... 114
VII.—THEORY OF PREPARATION FOR PREACHING, 131
VIII.—DELIVERY IN PREACHING, ... 173
IX.—FRAGMENTS OF THOUGHT, ... 206

    I.—OPTIMISM, ... 206
    II.—THE DIVINE PURPOSES, ... 211
    III.—MYSTERY, ... 218
    IV.—HAPPINESS, ... 222
    V.—SIN, ... 226
    VI.—THE REIGN OF SIN, ... 231
    VII.—MERCY, ... 237
    VIII.—THE REDEEMER, ... 244
    IX.—THE WORK OF THE SPIRIT, ... 251
    X.—MEDIATION, ... 256
    XI.—JUSTIFICATION BY GRACE, ... 262
    XII.—FAITH, ... 269
    XIII.—CHARACTER OF BELIEVERS, ... 275
    XIV.—TRUTH THE SAME AND ALWAYS YOUNG: THE OLD IN THE NEW, ... 283

I.

MIRACLES THE PROOF OF CHRISTIANITY.

1. SIDE by side with the recent naturalistic ideas of Christianity, have come, as might have been expected, objections to miracles as proof of it. There is a reason why the objections and the ideas should be found together: the natural in the religion can have no need of, or affinity with, the supernatural or miraculous in the evidence. Hume opposed miracles because he thought, that admitting them, they proved Christianity; our naturalists oppose them because, as they allege, they are unnecessary, if not a hindrance, to its proof. The difference is only in appearance: the naturalists agree with Hume in opposing miracles; they do not really disagree with him as to the bearing of miracles on the proof of Christianity. What the naturalists call Christianity did not in Hume's time pass under that name; it would not, in itself, have been unacceptable to him, only he would have thought it a misnomer to call it Christianity.

2. To determine whether miracles are necessary to the proof of Christianity—our present undertaking—

the meaning of the terms must be fixed. Understanding by Christianity, a revelation distinctively and directly from God ; and by miracles, direct works of God, wrought in attestation of it, our inquiry is : Are the latter the proper proof of the former ? Or, may Christianity be adequately proved without miracles ? A miracle, according to its etymology, sometimes signifies what is simply wonderful or marvellous ; sometimes it is what is supposed to be *superhuman;* sometimes it is something *supernatural*, or out of the order, if not an arrest and inversion of the order of nature, and unexplainable by any law, at least any known law of nature. In our use of the word, a miracle is a direct work of God, performed in nature and under the notice of the senses, but of divine, in contradistinction to natural or finite force. God, indeed, is in a true sense the force of nature's forces ; still there are works which God does not, and works which he does, directly and personally perform ; and miracles, as we take the term, are divine works of the latter class. We assume, as out of question, that the testimonial miracles of Christianity are DIRECT OR PERSONAL WORKS OF GOD.

We would state more precisely what we take to be the true idea of revelation as actualized in Christianity. According to Westcott,* the objects of revelation are " things essentially existing beneath the suffering, sin, and disorder, which are spread over the world within us and without ;" and revelation itself is " the removal of the dark veil from the face of these things ;"

* *Introduction to the Study of the Gospels*, p. 34.

that is to say, if we understand him, revelation acquaints us with nothing extra-natural or out of the sphere of nature; it only removes a veil from what exists essentially in "man and nature"—the world within us and without. We do not accept this view of the objects, or the office of revelation. The Scripture revelation does more than remove a veil from things essentially existing in the world; it acquaints us, by direct communication from God, with things not existing in the world; even the deep, the infinite things of God, of which, independently of this revelation, no one would have had an idea, though all the secrets of nature had been disclosed to him. There are things, indeed, presupposed and embodied in those of revelation, doctrines and precepts of natural religion, facts of history, which are not peculiar to it; these things do not individuate the revelation, or distinguish it as such; some of the distinctive things are: the Trinity of Persons in the unity Divine Essence; the Divine-human character of Jesus of Nazareth; the salvation of mankind by the blood and intercession of the Lord Jesus; the resurrection of the same body; these are peculiarities of revealed religion; they are not things lying under a dark veil spread over the face of the world, but things altogether *extra-mundane*, having no place in man or nature, the world within us or without. The idea of revelation, according to which nothing is revealed except what previously existed in the world under a veil, seems to Westcott " to be peculiarly Christian;" we reject it, as identifying substantive Christianity with natural religion.

3. Our limits allow us but a word on the arguments against miracles. Hume contented himself with assailing their *reality*, or trying to make out the impossibility of *proving* them. Miracles, he insisted, are contrary " to firm and unalterable experience ;" which, surely, he was safe enough in saying no testimony can countervail.* But how did he know what he asserts as a fact? Whether miracles are against all experience, is the point in question. His task was not to assert, but to prove the affirmative ; a task he has evaded. A host of unimpeachable witnesses has affirmed the occurrence of miracles as a matter of their own experience. Hume has not discredited their testimony,† which, if it cannot be discredited, disproves his assumption ; he is mistaken as to the reality of the ground of his argument.—Recently it has been alleged in the interest of Hume's attempt, that the testimony for miracles can be no other than testimony to sensible events seemingly miraculous ; that they were really miracles, could have been to the spectators only a matter of belief, not of experience. But the witnesses of miracles were not the spectators of them only: the prime witnesses were the performers of them, who wrought them, as they declared, in the

---

* " A miracle is a violation of the laws of nature ; and as a firm and unalterable experience has established these laws, the proof against a miracle, from the very nature of the fact, is as entire as any argument from experience can possibly be imagined."—*Essay on Miracles*, p. 160.

† He has said, indeed, that there is not to be found in all history any trustworthy testimony to miracles, but he has *said* it merely. (See *Essay on Miracles*, p. 163.)

name, and simply as instruments in the hand of God. Theirs, chiefly, is the testimony to be discredited. "If St. Paul did not work actual, sensible, public miracles, he has knowingly in these letters," says Paley, "borne his testimony to a falsehood." Did St. Paul, with his fellow-apostles and others, bear such testimony in fact?

Modern naturalists, going further than Hume, deny not the reality or demonstrableness only, but the *possibility* of miracles. Science, they say, has discovered that order in the world is a pure necessity, and absolutely inviolable; but science can have made no such discovery as this, unless it has further discovered that the world is not the creature of God, or is independent of him; or, in a word, that there is no God distinct from the world. If the world with its order be the creature of God, the order in it may be necessary and inviolable in respect of creatures, but surely not in respect of God himself, who is no longer God if he cannot destroy or change as well as establish a certain order. If it be said that he is, by nature, the God of order, this, though doubtless true in the highest sense of the term order, does not imply that miracles are against order in that sense. For aught we know they may not be, and the assertion that they are, is an assertion merely. "Once believe that there is a God," says Paley, "and miracles are not incredible."

4. But now to our question. Assuming that miracles are both possible and real, may Christianity be adequately proved without them? We take Christi-

anity as a revelation in the sense already expressed. In any other view of it, miracles, among proofs of Christianity, would, as we have already intimated, be superfluous if not obtrusive. "Those," says Mansell, "who deny the existence of any special revelation of religious truths distinct from that general sense in which mere reason itself, and all that it can discover, are the gifts of Him from whom every good thing comes, are only consistent when they deny that miracles have any value as evidences of religious truth; and are still more consistent when they deny that such works have been wrought." How gratuitous, and therefore how improper to work miracles in attestation of things essentially existing in the world! To remove the veil, to show the things, would be to prove them: if they and Christianity were identical, the latter would doubtless be self-demonstrative apart from all external evidence. The truth, revealed through Christ, would have, as Coleridge affirms it has, its evidence in itself. Infinitely different is Christianity, according to the meaning in which our question takes the term. It uses the term in its own signification when it asks whether Christianity can be adequately attested without miracles.

5. And now, first of all, let us understand what is an *adequate* attestation, a sufficient proof of Christianity? This, if we mistake not, is determinative of the main question. Whatever the requisite proof may be, one thing is certain, that Christianity is not sufficiently attested if its evidence does not justify and demand, not a persuasion of the possibility or proba-

bility, but a full undoubting assurance of the absolute verity of its averments : not that this assurance must or always does attend the evidence, which, through preoccupation may be neglected, or through prejudice, misjudged ; but that it is demanded *by the nature of the evidence.* Christianity itself makes this demand of mankind : Wherever it comes it holds itself entitled to immediate acceptance as true and as divine ; proclaims a fearful menace to unbelief, the menace of eternal death ; it imputes to unbelief the highest criminality, even that of making God himself a false witness ; it connects this infinite guilt with every degree of unbelief, so that he who believes with an incomplete faith is ready, with a penitence proportional to his shortcoming in faith, to cry out, with the father of the lunatic child : " Lord, I believe, help thou my unbelief." It has been said* that the assent to which Christianity is entitled is not equal to that which we owe to the discoveries of science ; that a sense of probability is the utmost the former can legitimately include, while the latter must extend to a sense of certainty. But how inadvertent or disloyal to the interests of Christianity is this remark ! Well has Stillingfleet said, that " an assent no stronger than to a thing merely probable, which is that it may or may not be true, is not properly assent at all, but a suspension of our judgment till some convincing argument be produced on either side."† But confront this remark with the peremptory claim of Christianity to

---

* In *Aids to Faith,* Essay II.   † *Origines Sacræ,* vol. i., p. 222.

our absolute assent. According to this claim, what is there that ought to be more certain to me than the truth of Christianity? Not the existence of God, or the existence of the world, or my own existence. "He who believeth not is condemned already, because he hath not believed;" "he hath made God a liar." This fact it is that gives the answer to the question, as to the nature of the proof, that adequately authenticates Christianity. The assent required is surely not out of proportion to the proof. The measure of the first is not greater than the measure of the second. The contrary supposition charges the highest injustice on him who only is just and good. "If there be no evidence given sufficient to carry the minds of men beyond mere probability, what sin can it be in those who cannot be obliged to believe as true what is only discovered as probable?"* On the ground of this postulate, then, let our inquiry proceed. Abstract the miracles, and will there be adequate proof of Christianity?

6. But before advancing let us name one preliminary more, and one bearing with decisive force on the decision of our question. The miracles are in fact innumerable, and they have never been separated from Christianity. Whether the proof of our religion required miracles or not there has been no experiment to determine. Christianity has never existed except, as we may say with emphasis, in the blaze of miracles. Revealed religion, itself a miracle, was accompanied at its beginning with testimonial miracles, to which

* *Stillingfleet*, vol ii., p. 222.

others were added, from time to time throughout the whole history of its progress. What a brilliant galaxy of miracles in days of old before the advent of Christ! How full of splendid miracles the life-history of our Lord! How is the record of the beginning and planting of Christianity studded with miracles as the firmament with stars! But more, much more than this: miracles are not only accompaniments of Christianity, they are inwrought and consubstantial with it. "Miracles and prophecy," says Rothe, "are not adjuncts appended from without to a revelation independent of them, but are constitutive elements of the revelation itself." "The miracles in the Bible," Bolingbroke has said, "are not like those in Livy, detached pieces that do not disturb the civil history, which goes on very well without them. But the whole history is founded on them; it consists of little else, and if it were not a history of them it would be a history of nothing." "Miracles," says Mansell, "are part of the *moral* as well as sensible evidences, and cannot be denied without destroying both kinds of evidence alike. 'That ye may know that the Son of Man hath power on earth to forgive sins, I say unto thee arise and take up thy couch and go into thine house.' 'If I with the finger of God cast out devils, no doubt the kingdom of God is come among you.' 'By the name of Jesus Christ of Nazareth, even by him, doth this man stand before you whole:' Let us imagine, for an instant, such words as these to have been uttered by one who was merely employing a superior knowledge of natural laws to produce a false appearance of supernatural power; by an astronomer, for instance, who had predicted an eclipse to a crowd of savages; or by a chemist availing himself of his science to exhibit *relative* miracles to an ignorant people, and we shall feel at once how even the most natural explanation of miraculous phenomena deals the death-blow to the *moral character* of the teacher no less than to the sensible evidence of his mission." We see then how the miraculous enters essentially into the very constitution and structure of Christianity. In fact, it can no more be separated from either the intrinsic or the testimonial, the moral or sensible evidence of Christianity, than color from the rainbow, or light from the rays of the sun. Whether, then, miracles were or were not necessary, they have never been wanting. In number, almost without number, they do, in fact, attest Christianity. And this decides one thing, and it is the only thing needed to justify the high claim of our religion, this, namely, that, taking the evidence of Christianity as it in reality is, there can be no question as to its sufficiency; *with* its miracles it is sufficient, whether it would or would not be *without* them. There is no ground of certainty if there be none in this evidence: it is no less infallible than the character of God. The presence of miracles is the presence of God himself as a Deponent. Unbelief in Christianity does, indeed, make God a false witness: there is no deeper criminality. "When He is come, He will reprove the world of sin, because they believe not on me."

7. But though miracles are in fact inseparable

from the evidences of Christianity, their absence may be imagined; and there are those who, as apologists for Christianity, say they would prefer their absence, and would fain eliminate them, if they could; and groundless and purposeless as our question may now seem, the cause of Christianity, as claiming to be a revelation directly from God, is staked on the decision of it. The answer to this question tests the naturalistic view of revealed religion. If there is no necessity for the miraculous in the evidence, it is because there is nothing miraculous in the religion : in our sense of the term it is not a revelation. Away with miracles, means, away with a so-called miraculous revelation. The inquiry whether Christianity may not be proved without miracles, is virtually the inquiry whether essential Christianity may not be resolved into naturalism. Let us then proceed.

8. If Christianity can be proved apart from testimonial miracles, it must be either by the self-evident truthfulness of its substantive or constitutive elements; or by its moral evidence; or by its proper effects; or lastly, its collateral evidences, so-called, in counterdistinction to miracles, will suffice to prove it. We are to inquire whether, *without any pre-supposition or aid of the miraculous*, sufficient evidence may be derived from these sources.

Is Christianity its own witness through its individuality as a revelation, or its constitutive elements? " Evidences of Christianity!" says Coleridge, " I am weary of the word." " The truth revealed through Christ has its evidence in itself." Let us patiently inquire as to the fact concerning this: Has Christianity *its evidence in itself?* We have distinguished, in Christianity, between what it has in common with natural religion, and what is distinctively its own. The present question has no reference to the former; so far as that is concerned, the evidence is in itself; but it is no part of the evidence of Christianity, as such, being no part, distinctively, of Christianity itself. It is in respect to the latter that we ask, does it, apart from miracles, or by *mere self-evidence,* assert its own truth? The things concerning which we inquire, whether they are self-evident or not, are of the class including the following: That the Eternal Word was made flesh in the Person of Jesus; that the death of Jesus was the redemption of the world; that Jesus is the Almighty Ruler and Judge of the world; that the dead will be raised by him at the last day: are these things, independently of testimony, true to the reason of mankind? The question gives its own answer. "Nothing," says Dr. Hodge, "in the apprehension of rationalists, can be more absurd than that the blood of the cross can remove sin." "We preach Christ crucified," said Paul, "to the Jews a stumbling-block, and to the Greeks foolishness." The Gospel certainly never made its way by recommending itself to the intuitive consciousness, or the natural reason, of man, apart from external evidences of its truth. No more palpably untrue assertion could be made than that Christianity, in its supernatural peculiarities, has its evidence in itself, meaning thereby that it has no need of external proof. "There is nothing," says Calvin, "that is more at variance with human reason than this article of our faith (the resurrection of the body). For who but God alone could pursuade us that bodies which are now liable to corruption, will, after having rotted away, or after they have been consumed by fire, or torn in pieces by wild beasts, not only be restored entire, but in a greatly better condition? Do not all our apprehensions of things reject this as a thing fabulous, nay, the greatest absurdity in the world?" Truly, only God himself, bearing witness directly to the truth of Christianity, could justify or warrant belief in it. Reason, nature itself, demands that God himself, by supernatural works, or some equivalent means, attest a supernatural revelation, such as Christianity claims to be. They are its natural and proper proofs. "I should not be a Christian," said St. Augustine, "but for miracles." Except for miracles, there would not have been sin in not believing on Jesus Christ. "If I had not done among them the works which none other man did, they had not had sin." Claiming to be the Messiah, it behooved our Lord to authenticate His claim by miracles—preännounced notes of Messiahship—which, if He had not wrought, the Jews, in reverence of the prophetic Scriptures, ought to have rejected Him. Let us inquire, then, of those who say that Christianity has its evidence in itself, what they mean by this language. Taking Christianity, with its concreted testimonial miracles, it has its evidence in itself, and witnesses in its own behalf, as the sun does for himself, by the light and heat which he sheds through the world ; but apart from the evidence of miracles, ought it not to be discredited ?

9. It is demonstrated, it has been said, by its moral evidence, or ethical excellency. Is this so ? We have seen that the moral in the evidence is, in fact, interblended and consubstantiated with the miraculous; but still it is urged that the moral, of itself, and without need of the miraculous, demonstrates the truth of Christianity. The ethics of Christianity stamp it, beyond all question, as Divine. And as a general fact, is it not the ethical influence, or the moral evidence of Christianity, that, as the objective cause, actually produce faith in men ?—Be it so—we assent not only, but affirm and insist. It cannot be denied that Christianity, to one susceptible of the specific impressions from it, does witness for itself, does demonstratively assert its divinity, by its ethical peculiarity. In such a type, and with such resplendence, has the ethical element been developed in Christianity, as to make it an absolute Unique in the earth ; and challenge for it, wherever it is known, the assent of the world, as a miraculous revelation. And this evidence it truly is, that in every case prevails, in actually gaining men's assent to Christianity, so far as it is gained in truth. None, at least, become true believers while they are insensible to the moral evidence, the ethical or spiritual excellency of the Gospel. All the evidences pour their force into the moral, or become *moralized*, so to speak, when that impress is given to the susceptible heart, which is the just counterpart, in man, of objective Christianity. To that spiritual dis-

cernment, in which faith has its upspring and being, all the things of the Spirit of God are, preëminently, ethical things;—permeated and filled with the fulness of ethical power and excellency. Well does Edwards resolve "a spiritual and saving conviction of the truth and reality of the things revealed in the word of God" into "a sense of the divine excellency (the moral glory) of these things." Nevertheless the evangelical morality, that form of morality which constitutes the moral evidence and asserts the truth of Christianity, so far from being without the miraculous, has the miraculous in fact, as its suppositum and ground. It is a form or type of morality, taken altogether from the contact and intercourse of the principle of morality with the miraculously attested wonders of redemption. The moral evidence of Christianity, distinctively, is not its embodiment of morality in the abstract, or of morality in so far as it is common between Christianity and natural religion, but that peculiar and ineffably glorious type of morality, which consists in the concretion of the ethical element in the miraculous facts of the great mystery of Godliness: God manifest in the flesh, justified in the spirit, seen of angels, preached unto the nations, believed on in the world, received up into glory. It could not be known that Christianity is Divine or truthful in its claims to divinity from morality unmodified by influences from its own facts and doctrines: no such exhibition or enforcement of morality could avail, in any degree, to prove the Trinity in God, or the incarnation of the Word, or the atonement, or the resurrection.

In order to be demonstrative by its moral evidence, Christianity with its supernatural wonders, must come itself into the sphere of morality, and take a form of morality from itself, and express itself in that form; that is to say, produce a morality distinctively *Christian;* or such as has Christianity, with its miracles, for its origin and base. It is divinely revealed and attested Christian truth, that entering into the ethical sphere, makes all things there new, giving every principle a new illustration, and every precept a new exposition and a new motive, and making every man who becomes an example of it, a new creature—this is the moral evidence which demonstrates Christianity. It has its breath and being in the miracles; take them away, and the evidence goes with them. Apart from these, the ethical superiority of Christianity is, so far, to its praise, but does not demonstrate its claims to a divine origin.

10. Next, is there proof of Christianity from its effects, or actual efficiency on mankind, apart from miracles? We do not ask whether this evidence is demonstrative, but whether the influence of miracles is to be excluded from it. The evidence *is* demonstrative: the tree is known by its fruits—Christianity meets the infinite wants of man; it recovers him from the dominion of sin; it creates him anew in the image of God; it is the power of God unto salvation to every one who believes in it. Here truly is the crowning evidence of the truth of Christianity, and it is evidence which Christianity will always be multiplying to itself. But the present question is, Does this evidence

imply that miracles may be dispensed with? And the answer to it is, that the evidence is the very fruitage of miracles. Whence that efficacy of Christianity which supplies this evidence? What is this efficacy but that of a wondrous miracle, or collection of miracles, enshrined in countless witnessing miracles? Would a Christianity, so called, denuded of the miraculous, have had the same efficacy? Take away this element from the Gospel, and would it still be the perfect satisfaction of human need, the power of God unto salvation?

11. As yet, then, we have no proof of Christianity, apart from miracles. May it not, nevertheless, be sufficiently proved without them, by its collateral evidence? We have already answered this question. Christianity has evidence of this kind of an immense amount, in which apparently or distinctively, there is nothing of the miraculous. "It has pleased the Divine Author of our religion," says Mansell, "to fortify his revelation with evidence of various kinds, appealing with different degrees of force to various minds, and to the same mind at different times." In the words of Butler, "the evidence of Christianity is a long series of things reaching as it seems from the beginning of the world to the present time, of great variety and compass." Is there not in this series of things evidence enough to prove Christianity independently of the miraculous portion of it? Butler, who ascribes great weight to this evidence, "consisting of things not reducible to the heads, either of miracles or the completion of prophecy,"

still, while making these two the direct and fundamental proofs, adds that those others (the collateral proofs), however considerable they are, ought *never to be urged apart from the direct proofs, but to be always joined with them.*" Why should the collateral proofs never be urged apart from the direct ones, but always be joined with them? For two palpable reasons: first, because, if the collateral proofs could exist, apart from the direct, they would not be in themselves or in their influence, equivalent to the direct. They would not be, as God himself directly deposing to the truth of Christianity, so as to make unbelief an impeachment of the veracity of God: the evidence of Christianity must be this, or equivalent to this; miracles are the thing itself, the collateral proofs are neither the thing nor its equivalent. What they would amount to by themselves as demanding assent, what measure of assent they would call for, or justify, if perfectly appreciated, we cannot determine; but the very fact, if it were a fact, that such miraculous matters as those of substantive Christianity had no miraculous attestation, would, as we have seen, apart from posterior requisitions, be such a presumption against its truth, as no evidence could overcome. Reason—nature itself, would, to the last, require that attestation. Christianity, without it, would be incredible.—But secondly, the collateral evidences should not be urged apart from the direct or miraculous, because separate from the latter they have, and can have, in fact, no existence. The collateral evidences, like every thing in Christianity, had their origin and source in the miraculous, are an outflow from it, and can in reality be no more separated from it, or used in proof against its necessity, than beams of sunlight be separated from, and then made an argument against, the necessity of the body of the sun. It is owing to miracles originally and determinantly, that the collateral evidences are what they are. We know not what would have been the course of things in the history of Christianity, had it not originated and started in miracles: enough that we know what was the fact: the success of Christianity, the conversion of the Roman empire, the lives of the saints, the testimony of the noble army of martyrs, the progress of civilization and the arts under Christian institutions and society, the whole of that long series of things reaching from the beginning of the world to the present time, which comprehends all the collateral proofs of Christianity,—instead of implying that miracles are not necessary as direct proofs of it, infer the reality, if not the necessity also of miracles, as certainly as the fruit and foliage of a tree infer the reality of the tree. Well, therefore, has Butler said, the collateral should never be urged apart from the direct proofs of Christianity, but be always joined with them. Most fitly and undeniably has this other important word been spoken by the same great author: "Revelation itself is miraculous, and miracles are the proof of it." The collateral evidences, apart from miracles, are not the proof of it, and as such should never be urged or relied on.

12. But after all, how are miracles the supreme,

ultimate, decisive Test of the truthfulness of Christianity, since miracles themselves are amenable to a test? Be it that they are decisive, that they give absolute certainty, when once their genuineness is beyond doubt: still if there are true miracles, there are also false ones; and there is evidence which, if it be against a miracle, no miracle can countervail; that, namely, of self-evident truth and goodness. We know from Scripture itself (see Deut. xiii. 1–11) that if the object or purpose of a miracle be wrong, the testimony of the purpose against the miracle is stronger than the testimony of the miracle, or any miracle can be, in the interest of the purpose. And does it not hence follow that miracles, instead of proving Christianity, are dependent on Christianity for their own proof? that if we know the miracles to be true, we know this, because we know by antecedent and higher evidence, the religion to be true? This argument seems to have convinced some persons that the defence of Christianity is complete, independent of the testimony of miracles, and is rather impeded than facilitated by it.

13. But the argument is a fallacy. It assumes as true in an absolute sense, what is true only in a certain case. Because a miracle, so called, wrought for a bad purpose, is already condemned by its purpose, it concludes that every miracle depends for its credibility on knowledge of its purpose; or, in ignorance of its purpose, is necessarily undeterminative as to its own genuineness. It cannot assert its own reality as a miracle, a personal or direct work of God, unless it is

known to what intent it is wrought. The argument is, that since a bad purpose condemns an alleged miracle performed in its favor, no miracle, irrespective of acquaintance with its purpose, can, as a miracle, authenticate itself. The sophistry is manifest. It is a mere truism, that no miracle can countervail the contradictory testimony of a *bad* purpose or object; it is simply asserting that a true miracle cannot be wrought in attestation of a *bad* purpose; that God cannot act, cannot exert his power in the interest of moral evil; that is to say, cannot deny or undeify Himself. But does this imply that He can never act and authenticate the act as His own, unless it is already known why or to what intent the act is performed? Must we know what God intends by His works, before we can be certain that the works are indeed His? Can He do no works capable of differencing themselves absolutely from the works of His creatures? We know that He can have no bad design; we know that He must have some design, not unworthy of Himself; but must He acquaint us with His designs, before He can perform works which shall be able to assert themselves as distinctively His own? It is true that we know not the limit of finite power; but cannot infinite power go beyond that limit, and there put itself forth in works after its own kind, which no finite power shall be able to equal, or successfully counterfeit? And by such self-authenticated works, cannot God authenticate a revelation which, as such, could not otherwise be adequately attested? What if we knew no more as to the purpose of Christianity than that it is not a bad one, or one unworthy of the Deity? might not God, without acquainting us further with its object, seal it as a revelation, by incontestable miracles? May this be denied, without limiting the Holy One?

14. But we have been putting the matter at its greatest disadvantage. Our knowledge is not altogether negative as to the purpose of Christianity; its purpose is worthy of its miracles, and required them for its fulfilment; and whatever may be said of a supposed necessity or duty of testing or proving miracles, here are miracles which are their own proof. Admitting that the Scripture miracles were really wrought, we may as well deny that God made the world, as deny that He was their author. If the genuineness of some of them, apart from the rest, and from the system to which they all belong, might seem to be questionable, yet, as a whole, once admit their reality, and the possibility of reasonable doubt as to their authorship is excluded. If the plagues of Egypt, the giving of the manna, the crossing of the Jordan, the regression of the sun, the swimming of the iron, the walking on the sea, the resurrection of Lazarus, the resurrection of our Lord—if these, with the rest of the Scripture miracles, were matters of fact, he who, admitting them as such, does not believe in the religion which they attest, does indeed charge God Himself with bearing false witness. It is not because these miracles do not assert themselves to be miracles indeed, that there is held to be a necessity for superior or antecedent proof. The Creation itself is not more self-

evidently of God, than the testimonial miracles of Christianity.

15. Miracles, then — untestable, because there is nothing to test them by — miracles wrought, it is certain, for no *unworthy* purpose, but not dependent on a knowledge of their purpose for proof of their reality, are the direct, fundamental, indispensable proofs of Christianity. Whatever is peculiar in Christianity, would never have been known had it not been revealed, and for evidence of its truth, or its demonstrative certitude, rests at last on testimonial miracles. Except as ultimately assured by these divine vouchers, I have no sufficient ground for rational belief as to any thing distinctively or peculiarly Christian. I do not know that there are more Persons than one to whom Deity belongs, or that Jesus was God, or that His death was an atonement for the sins of mankind, or that the dead will be raised by Him; I do not know these things by intuition, or because, independently of external proofs, they are true to my reason; I know them because God, having revealed them by His Holy Spirit, has sealed that revelation by evidence either in itself directly miraculous, or having the miraculous first, last, and midst, as its ground.

16. After all, however, it may be objected that if Christianity behooved to certify itself by miracles, it behooved to continue miracles. To the masses of mankind, for whom Christianity was chiefly intended, historical miracles, as far as their ability to verify them is concerned, are as nothing. What, to the common people, as to power of verifying them to themselves, are events

of the far distant past? Moreover, as a general fact, it is notorious that men do not become Christians from personal examination of the testimony of miracles, or the historical evidences of Christianity. This objection is virtually answered already. The miracles, though performed ages ago, are present, and live in all the ages, and even to the unlearned and children, witness for Christianity to-day, not less decisively and strongly than they did at first. The Scripture miracles are not as other events of the past, in respect of the antiquating influence of time ; on the contrary, they and those events, are in this respect a contrast to one another. The miracles were not left, like common occurrences, to the accidents of tradition, or chance, or human history ; they were not detached, isolated, inorganic things ; they all pertained to one whole, with every part of which, as with the whole, they were co-organized, interconnected, and, as it were, interfused. The miracles of Christianity are, in fact, as we have already said, among its integrant, constitutive elements ; they live in its life ; they live in the Scriptures, in the Church, and in the holy examples and confession of members of the Church : in preaching, in the sacraments, in all the memorials and ordinances of Christianity, their witnessing presence and power are conserved and felt. Besides, the miracles of power which attest Christianity, are like Christianity itself, and whatever essentially belongs to it, is perpetually quickened and rejuvenated by another species of miracles, comprised in *the completion of the prophecies*—miracles of knowledge, which are continually being accomplished, as time advances in its course. These direct and fundamental proofs of Christianity, in their demonstrative force, enter into every part and fibre of the great organism which they authenticate as divine, and at once verify and are verified by it. In this sense, it is true that the religion asserts the miracles, as well as the miracles the religion. The proofs of Christianity, direct and collateral, "make up," to use the admirable words of Butler, "all of them together, one argument, the conviction arising from which kind of proof may be compared to what they call *the effect* in architecture, or other works of art—a result from a number of things so and so disposed, and taken into one view." The miracles are in the view with all the rest, attesting all, and in and through all, attesting and asserting themselves; and in their proper influence, no less, perhaps even more effective, on the whole, at this day, than they were to many who saw them performed. There is no need of new miracles; indeed, they might be a disadvantage, and, after a short time, would, in effect, cease to be miracles. If the old miracles, certified as they are to all, do not convince men, new ones doubtless would also fail to do it. "If they hear not Moses and the prophets"—if Moses and the prophets, with the miracles which attested and still attest their mission, are disregarded by them—"neither would they be persuaded though one rose from the dead." Greater, doubtless, to us, is the advantage from the Scripture miracles, greater as they lie together in the one view of which we have spoken; more decisive as evidencing the truth of revealed religion, than would be the repetition of fresh miracles every day. Miracles prove Christianity, but they may fail to make converts to it. Referring to the too common results of miracles, Pascal has said, "the purpose of miracles is not to convert, but to condemn."

17. The objection owes what of force it may seem to have, to great indiscrimination; it does not distinguish between what the evidence of Christianity behooves to be in itself, and the way and the degree in which it becomes effective in individual converts—between the necessity of its having a sufficient ground for its authoritative demand for faith, and the measures and workings of faith, on the part of those in whom the demand is met. To make the former complete, the specific testimony of miracles is necessary; the latter, though the influence of miracles, as before explained, is never wanting in it, vary indefinitely with different persons. In no one is faith commensurate with the objective demand for it; nor is it alike as to its origin and advances in all. St. Augustine, but for miracles historically verified, to and by himself, could not have been a Christian; the generality do not distinctively feel the necessity of miracles, or formally recognize their specific influence and function as the supreme Test and proof of Christianity. They also, in a true sense, would not believe, but for miracles, but it is the miraculous, as integrant and interfused in the whole of the evidence, and pervading the essence of Christianity, that their faith apprehends and rests in. It is the "one argument" of which But-

ler speaks, "made up of all the proofs taken together," the conviction arising from which he compares to what they call *the effect* in architecture, or other works of art. This it is that generally produces faith, when it becomes a personal reality. Different minds may be variously affected by it; some more by one part, some more by another; some in a larger, some in a smaller measure; but in every case, the efficiency of the whole, as such, is felt, and the result is the product of the whole. It is so from the fact that Christianity, with its proofs, is a single, living organism, each part of which interconnects itself with every other, giving every other part an influential, life-producing, if not a distinctly recognized presence.

18. This distinction between the fundamental necessity of miracles, as outward proofs or seals of testimony, and the influence of these and the other evidences in the genesis of faith, or in producing faith, in different persons, solves at once the objection before us. It was needful that the demonstration of Christianity should be absolute, irrespective of men's belief or disbelief; thus only could be justified its absolute claim to belief, and its denunciation of all unbelief. How it was to fare in the world, what fruit its evidence was to produce in the minds of men, or which part of the evidence was to be first or most effective, or what in the beginning and progress of a life of faith was to have ascendant power, depended on the different individualities of men, and the contingencies of time and circumstances.

19. On this point, it is to be further and distinctly

remembered, and strongly accented, that in every case of the subjective demonstration of Christianity, there is another agency concerned besides that of the outward evidence. It is not of themselves alone that men believe: faith is the gift of God. It is the inward demonstration of the Spirit and of power, that makes the external demonstration fruitful. Amidst the full effulgence of outward evidence, "if thine eye be evil, thy whole body will be full of darkness." Without the subjective prerequisites,—to use the words of Coleridge, without "that predisposing warmth, which renders the understanding susceptible of the specific impressions from the history, and from all other outward seals of testimony," the whole of the evidence, collateral and miraculous, internal and external, will be without avail, except to condemn, as Pascal said of the miracles, in particular. And it is also certain, and equally essential as bearing on the topic before us, that where the inward witnessing of the Spirit has place; where, to adopt Coleridge's language again, there is "a true efficient conviction of a moral truth—*the creation of a new heart*, which collects the energies of a man's whole being in the focus of the conscience," where there "is emphatically, that leading of the Father, without which no man can come to Christ," there the dominion of the entire external evidence is actualized. Christianity, now, has all its evidences at command, and they do their work. The miracles, whether distinctively verified or not, work together with all the rest. There is nothing now that does not bear witness to Christianity. Nature itself, under the power of this inward demonstration, this "one essential miracle," asserts the Supernatural :

> "Nature is Christian : preaches to mankind,
> And bids dead matter aid us in our creed."

20. On the whole, we are brought by the discussion we have been engaged in, to the conclusion that objections to miracles as proofs of Christianity presuppose and in fact have as their ground objections to veritable Christianity itself. As naturalism cannot but make objections to miracles as the proper proof of religion, so, reciprocally, when there are these objections, the religion adhered to, if any, is that of naturalism. An objector to miracles as proof of doctrine, cannot be an intelligent believer in such a doctrine as that of a plurality of Persons in the God-head, or of the two Natures in Christ, or of the resurrection of the dead. He ought not to call himself a Christian ; not even a *neo*-christian, unless he intend by the prefix to deny that he is a real Christian at all. The only religion which, after discarding miracles as proofs, has any ground of credibility in it, is that which, in the words of the *Westminster Review*, has its attestation "in the essential unity and self consistency of our moral and spiritual nature, opening more and more with the progressive education of the race, to a consciousness of the fundamental laws on which it rests, and which we learn partly through mutual intercourse and sympathy, partly through the awakening influence of superior minds, on those that are less developed and advanced." We would not press the inexorable con-

sequences of a theory on those who shrink from them; all who disparage miracles, are not, we must hope, absolute naturalists, yet we cannot but stand in doubt, if not of the substantial loyalty to the cause of Christian truth, at least of the logical consistency, of those who say they would rather have Christianity without than with the miracles, or that the credibility of miracles depends on doctrine rather than the credibility of doctrine on miracles. Nor can we adopt the formula, as applicable to a supernatural revelation, that " the miracle must witness for itself and the doctrine must witness for itself, and then the first is capable of witnessing for the second."* We take Butler as complete; *Revelation itself is miraculous and miracles are its proof.* If miracles do indeed witness for themselves, that is to say, assert themselves, demonstratively, to be direct works of God, they can witness for that which to us, through our ignorance, does not witness for itself, if by the will of God, they are wrought for that end. Revelation, apart from testimonial miracles, does not witness for itself to us: in this isolation it would not be true to human reason. The proper statement is : " the miracle must witness for itself; the doctrine, apart from the miracle, does not witness for itself ; the first, by itself, must witness for the second." In the evidence of miracles all other evidence has its ground and its beginning. Without miracles Christianity is indemonstrable.

21. Before dismissing the subject we would reproduce, for the purpose of emphasising with a specific

* Trench.

reference, what has already been expressed with some particularity as to *the measure or fulness of the assent demanded by Christianity.* What we would further say on this point is, that, while this assent indicates the nature of the proof of Christianity, it indicates at the same time the proper task of a Christian apologist. Whatever may be the measure or form of men's belief or disbelief of Christianity, there can, as we have urged, be no question that the assent which with infinite authority it challenges of all, is that of unqualified, absolute, prompt assurance. Most assuredly therefore he who sets himself to defend Christianity, undertakes, if he knows what he is doing, to make out a sufficiency in its evidences to produce, not a conviction of the probability or bare credibility, but a conviction of the absolute certainty of its truth. He must present evidence proportional to the assent required. If he does not do this, his attempt is a failure. If he only gives reason for a preponderant conviction, a balance of probability, in favor of Christianity, or for an assent short of a full sense of the certainty of its truth, he has not defended Christianity; he has at best only approximated a defence of it. Without controversy Christianity cannot be defended, if its evidence be not in itself and to a just appreciation of it, absolutely demonstrative. The claims of Christianity to positive, undoubting belief, cannot be otherwise justified. "If," says Stillingfleet, "there be no evidences given sufficient to carry the minds of men beyond mere probability, what sin can it be in them to disbelieve who cannot be obliged to believe as true what is only discovered as probable?" Yet a recent writer* on the study of the evidences has said that to require certainty as the just result of the evidence of Christianity, is to require an assent out of proportion to the evidence: as if there might be evidence greater than the direct testimony of God. And have not defences of Christianity, so called, works on the evidences, too often contented themselves with this idea as the utmost which the evidence can extend to? And why, but from not thinking with Butler, or forgetting what he has said, that the collateral evidences ought never to be urged apart from the direct, the miraculous ones, but to be always joined with them? The collateral evidences, by themselves, would not warrant the assent demanded by Christianity; but keep the two kinds of evidences always united, let the witnessing virtue of miracles be as it is in truth retained in every part of the evidence; let all the evidence involve and rest upon miracles as its substratum, what then, as to the nature, the measure of the assent demanded by it? Does the evidence then come short of substantiating its claim to a sense of certainty, as its proper counterpart in man? Let men apprehend this as the fact respecting the evidence, and ought they to be less certain of the truth of Christianity than of that of natural science, or of the existence of the world, or of their own existence? In the words of Stillingfleet, we ask, " can there be greater evidence that a testimony is infallible, than that it is the testimony of God Himself?" Let us not disparage the books on the evi-

* *Aids to Faith.*

dences; there are among books few of greater power; they triumphantly refute all objections; they are victorious in all controversies; they do completely what they undertake to do; they overwhelm infidelity with its logical inconsistencies and absurdities; but after all, what for the most part have they achieved or aimed at in the battle of the evidences, but just to show the bare credibility of the religion attested by them? When a spiritual man, after pondering, doubtless not without edification and delight, the profound and masterly treatises of the apologists, comes into the presence of the great Object itself, in whose interest they labor so well, and looks directly upon the Miracle Christianity, encompassed by countless testimonial miracles, how feeble is language to express the difference of which he now becomes conscious, between the title of Christianity to assent, and the measure of assent which these works contend for? And whence the difference, if not from inappreciation of the place and position of miracles in the evidence? It is in two respects with the evidence of Christianity, as with that of the being of God; both are alike demonstrative in asserting the reality of their objects, and both alike unheeded or rejected, or dimly seen, even by the princes of human wisdom.

22. We add one remark. Is not a reässertion of the miraculous in the evidence of revealed religion an especial desideratum of the times? If it be possible, should not the Scripture miracles be made to reäppear as living realities, before the eyes of this generation? Otherwise where before long will be faith in revela-

tion? Natural religion, even, seems to be standing "a tiptoe," ready to forsake the sphere of religious philosophy. What more notorious, than that the religious philosophy of the day is mainly pantheistic? "It is an admitted fact," said Isaac Taylor some years since, "that already all, or nearly all, educated men from end to end of continental Europe, those of the Anglo-Saxon race alone excepted, are either open pantheists, or are kept from avowing themselves to be so, by motives of conventional propriety, or of policy." The Anglo-Saxons themselves are becoming unsteadfast in belief in a Personal God. Men of high culture, English and American, are coming to the conclusion that there is no Divine Being different from the world, and nothing in a proper sense supernatural. Not many of these as yet profess themselves to be pantheists, but leading minds among them employ reasonings and forms of expression, which involve pantheism inevitably, and not obscurely or indirectly. It may be traced too perceptibly in some of the recent review articles. Professor Powell tells us that " to attempt to reason from law to volition, from order to active power, from universal reason to *distinct personality*, from design to self-existence, from intelligence to infinite perfection, is in reality to adopt grounds of argument and speculation entirely beyond those of strict philosophic inference." Pantheism on a large and increasing scale is the manifest goal to which modern thinking on religion is tending. The fact is on all sides seen and confessed. It is beginning to be felt beyond the educated classes; the people at large are becoming more or less acquainted and pleased with pantheistic speculations. What is to be done? Something surely besides what has been or what is being done. The means now and hitherto used have failed even to check the progress of the deadly error; it was never more triumphant than at the present moment. To what other means may we look? Shall we expect new theophanies, new manifestations of the supernatural and the miraculous, to confound the naturalism on all sides so predominant? What were this but to make incomplete or transitory the original attestation of Christianity; to make obsolete or invalid all the miracles both of the Old and New Testaments? What were it, moreover, but to make void our own highest responsibility and privilege; to cease from personal dignity and worth; to distrust and count as nothing the indwelling power and grace of the Holy Spirit; in short, to require *unnecessary* miracles; that is, in principle, to put miracles among common things; to make them indeed miracles no longer? This were virtually to become pantheists ourselves. Still the living reality, the influential presence of the miraculous in the evidence of Christianity, the just antitheton of naturalistic tendencies and successes,— this is clearly indicated and imperatively demanded, as their proper remedy. Never more than in this our day, should the "City of our God" be known and read of men by its name, JEHOVAH-SHAMMAH, THE LORD IS THERE. It will not be so known and read without direct, infallible revelations of the Divine Presence. "Out of Zion the perfection of beauty," the excellent glory itself must shine, and it will not shine thence, except in its own proper manifestations; the natural, simply, does not directly reveal, does not attest the Infinite or Divine. Naturalism will be efficiently confuted by nothing but an actual exhibition and perception of the miraculous, the proper seal of God. It is far from being certain that the presence of the miraculous would impart that perception of it; but its presence, its essential or influential presence, is necessary. All just religious conviction, all true piety, consists essentially in a sense of divinity or the miraculous as at once inhering in and attesting revelation; the central Miracle Christianity, authenticated as directly of God by its accompanying testimonial miracles. And may this sense be produced in the absence of its objective cause, the miraculously attested Miracle itself? Must not that Miracle by some means display itself anew? And by what other means, since new miracles are not to be looked for but by reasserting, producing anew, the testimony of the ancient miracles? But how is this to be done? Is it a possibility? Can Christianity, after eighteen centuries, reproduce its miraculous attestations as at first? The question has been answered. Christianity, in itself, or as an objective reality, has its first life always; its facts, its doctrines, its testimony, all live in, perpetuate, and are perpetuated by that life: therefore nothing in substantive Christianity can become stale or obsolete; by its constitutive elements, it is like its Author, in respect of time, the same yesterday, to-day, and forever: so it is in itself, and so it seems to be to every one whose understanding has been opened to understand it. To the eye of faith, Christianity is as novel, as wonderful now as it was to the disciples on the day of Pentecost. If in the primitive vigor and fruitfulness of faith Christianity should reappear in the life of the Church, would there be any decrepitude, any wrinkle or infirmity of age, any trace of the wear or waste of time in its aspect? The doctrines, the examples, and with all the rest, the miracles, would they not live again, as before the very eyes of men?* Would not this be the certain, the necessary consequence, even if to the miracles distinctively no special attention were drawn? But as the times call with such emphasis for the specific witness of miracles, as it is specially characteristic of the times to disown and deny God's direct testimony to His revelation, so abundantly given, and this for the reason that His revelation itself is disbelieved—this fact would make it impossible to the

---

* "Methought I saw, with great evidence, from the four evangelists, the wonderful works of God in giving Jesus Christ to save us, from His conception and birth even to His second coming to judgment; *methought I was as if I had seen Him born, as if I had seen Him grow up, as if I had seen Him walk through this world from the cradle to the cross.* . . . When I have considered also the truth of His resurrection, and have remembered that word, 'Touch me not, Mary,' etc., *I have seen as if He had leaped out of the grave's mouth,*'" etc. (*Bunyan's Life.*) See also Chrysostom on Gal. iii. 1 : " It was not in the country of the Galatians, but in Jerusalem, that He was crucified : how then does he (Paul) say *among you?* To demonstrate the power of faith, which is able to see even distant objects. And he does not say, ' was crucified,' but ' was painted crucified,' showing that by the eyes of faith they beheld more distinctly than some who were present and saw the transactions."

revived Church not to have a very prominent reference in all the workings of her life, inward and outward, in her thoughts, her prayers, her discourses, her books, the labors of her ministry, to the reproduction of the miraculous testimony, the sign-manual of God Himself. And the result would be sure: with corresponding prominence, the miracles would return and take their proper position among the evidences. The constancy of nature is not less to be doubted than that rejuvenated Christianity, novel and fresh as at first, with the advantage of an experience as old as time and not older than opulent in teachings of Divine wisdom and prudence, would renew its pristine demonstrativeness and power; and if still confronted by adversaries, of whatever number or whatever name, —neo-christians, naturalists, pantheists, atheists,— would by their opposition, however maintained, be no more retarded in its triumphant advances, than the sun is retarded in his circuit of the heavens by the mists and vapors of the atmosphere. "Woe unto him that striveth with his Maker. Let the potsherds strive with the potsherds of the earth."

II.

NATURE OF THE ATONEMENT.—I.

NOTHING is more emphatically taught in Scripture,* than that "the grace of God which bringeth salvation" could not have been bestowed arbitrarily, or without regard to principles of fitness and propriety, as to the MODE of procedure; but was under the highest necessity of adhering to a suitable manner in accomplishing its object. God, though above every other necessity, could not disregard His own character nor act in a way unworthy of Himself, as the Lord and Maker of all. Such a way is conceivable, but it was not possible, because not consistent with the essential perfections of the Divine Nature. It would not have *become* the Most High.

2. It may have been well, if not necessary, *on our account also*, that respect should have been had to method. The way of showing favor is itself often of more value than all particular benefits; indeed, essential to the permanent value of every benefit. A family may have received a father's generosity in the amplest measures, and yet be less indebted to him for this,

* Heb. ii. 10, 14, 17. Gal. iii. 21, etc.

than for his having always bestowed his offices of kindness in such a way as to make them so many instances of wisdom in himself — so many exemplary lessons to his household, as to the paramount value of character. It is often better that things in themselves very desirable should be left undone, rather than be done in an improper manner. Might not, then, the Divine favor towards man have proved no favor in the end, if God had disregarded mode in conferring it?

3. It was not only well, but absolutely indispensable *for our sakes*, that method should have been observed. Had not God consulted his own honor, He would not ultimately have benefited mankind. God is Himself the portion of man; but God dishonoring Himself were no more God. No happiness, no possibility of it, would be left to man, if God should do an unwise thing, or a thing on any account misbecoming the Supreme Majesty of heaven and earth. The benevolence of God, His power to bless mankind, depends on His always acting worthily of Himself.

4. But the Scripture* teaches that the glory of God, "the essential perfections of the Divine nature,"† required, that He should not only have had respect to manner, but have limited Himself to *one* manner namely, "the making the Captain of our salvation per-

---

* In the text before referred to and others.

† See Heb. ii. 10. We have not exaggerated the force of the word "*became*" in this passage. "The word signifies that decency and becomingness, which justice, reason and equity require ; so that the contrary would be unmeet, because unequal and unjust. Thus every one's duty, that which is incumbent on him,

fect through sufferings." For this—this, and no other—the necessity was the same as that God be unchangeably God, a Being of infinite perfection, who will not dishonor Himself by conduct unbecoming or unsuitable in such a Being.

5. The doctrine we are to explain, takes for granted concerning this plan, that it embraces what evangelical theology has termed AN ATONEMENT FOR SIN. By this phrase is intended, an amende, a compensation, or satisfaction, *for the remission or setting aside* of the condign punishment of sin; or the punishment of the sinner according to his desert. The idea of Atonement is sometimes identified with simple *at-one-ment*, or reconciliation; but if the design be to exclude what has now been expressed, it will not be pretended that this is the evangelical or orthodox meaning of the term. The Atonement, as commonly held by the Church, rests on the assumptions that man is a sinner, and that there is in the nature of sin that which deserves and calls for punishment; and is something which comes in place of punishment, supposing this to be forborne. Our object does not require us to examine the assumptions just mentioned. Taking as conceded, that man is a sinner, and that sin incurs punishment, we are to show the principles or nature of that Atonement or satisfaction for the remission of

in his place and station, is that which *becomes* him; and thence in the New Testament, that which is not κατα το πρεπον, thus decent, is condemned as evil, 1 Cor. xi. 13; 1 Tim. ii. 10: and itself is condemned as a rule of virtue, Mat. iii. 15; Eph. v, 3."—*Dr. Owen, in loc.*, Works, vol. iii. *p.* 394.

punishment, which, we assume, the way of the Divine mercy to mankind embraces.

6. We ground the necessity for an atonement, under the circumstances supposed, in the perfection of the Divine Nature, and the necessity that God always act worthily of Himself. Supposing that there is forgiveness with Him,—that He may and does remit the punishment of sin, God, we say, owes it to Himself, as the Best and Greatest, the Lord and Creator of all things, to require an atonement. Sin calls for punishment, and God cannot disregard the demand; cannot—if it be necessary that the Deity retain the glory of His nature inviolate. Of this the proof is in itself. The difference between good and evil, holiness and sin, is essential and immutable, and to this difference, no upright being can be insensible; neither can such a being refrain, if occasion arise, from expressing appropriately, approbation of holiness, and hatred of sin. The Most High, then, infinite as He is in moral perfection, and holding the provinces of Lawgiver and Ruler of the world, was under a necessity—that repeatedly mentioned, of being true to Himself in His mode of agency,—to manifest, in fitting measure and form, His disapprobation of sin. It became Him to do this, in the first place, in His Law—the rule of life which He gave to man; and, in the next place, he must do the same, if there be occasion, in administering and executing His Law. It is impossible, that either in the one or the other province, He should fail to express His estimate of the demerit or turpitude of sin; much more do, or omit to do, any-

thing, which might imply, that his His abhorrence of sin is less than it should be, or may be changed or abated. These things have their proof in themselves, and cannot be denied. But if they be true, how may God, acting towards His creatures as Lord and Judge of all, dispense with the punishment of sin? A penalty the law must have; and where it has been incurred by transgression, how may it consist with the moral rectitude of the Deity, not to execute the penalty? Is not punishment in this case necessary to the just revelation of the Divine displeasure against sin?

7. But the fact lies before us, and is admitted by all, that punishment is foreborne; that mercy in the Divine administration "rejoices against judgment," and opens the gates of Heaven to those who have incurred condemnation to eternal death. There is remission of punishment for rebellious men. But how might this take place, without dishonor to Him, "for whom are all things and by whom are all things?" The primary and natural means of maintaining His honor being set aside, does a possibility remain of securing the end by any other means? Our doctrine gives this question an affirmative reply. It asserts there was one other means,—namely, an *Atonement*, by which the end could be and was secured. And because the end must be secured, and could be by no other means, an Atonement in order to the forgiveness of mankind was as necessary, as that God do nothing incompatible with His essential excellency.

8. But how could even an Atonement answer the

purpose? The careful consideration of this question is necessary to our design. To see the truth distinctly here, is to understand the doctrine of the Atonement. Let it be remembered, then, what the precise thing was that would have put the Divine conduct out of harmony, out of consistency, with the essential perfection of God, in case of an arbitrary remission of punishment. It was just this, that there would in that case have been no appropriate revelation of the despleasure of God against sin. Against SIN: Not as jeoparding government merely, but as essentially evil in itself, apart from its actual or possible developments of its evil tendency. The interest of government does not comprehend the entire ground of the necessity for an Atonement. Does not the efficacy of the Atonement in maintaining government depend on its sufficiency to meet a higher demand, namely, that the harmony of the Divine Perfections be conserved, and particularly, that Justice, as an attribute of the Divine Nature, essential and indefeasible, irrespective of external relations and consequences, be satisfied? Let there be then an adequate revelation of God's displeasure against sin, and does not the necessity for punishment disappear? Why is punishment necessary any longer, if its object is attained? It was only in order to the manifestation of the Divine abhorrence of sin, that punishment was appointed. It was not appointed simply for its own sake. If it be possible, then, by any other means than punishment, to reveal in full measure and power the Divine Indignation against sin; in other words, if there be any means by which the end of punishment is answered as perfectly as by punishment itself, and if these means are provided, is not the way now open, so far as the honor of God is concerned, for the setting aside of punishment? May not pardoning mercy here intervene, and grace abound in all its offices of kindness and love, without opposition from any one of the Divine perfections? May not God now act as it becomes Him to do, even while He pours upon the guilty and the condemned, if only they are prepared to receive it, all the fulness of His benevolence? In the language of inspiration, may we not say that God now may be *just* and yet the justifier of men? Or is there still something in the nature of God inconsistent with the remission of punishment?

9. To some it appears, so at least we understand them to say, that *two* things in the Divine Nature are still inconsistent; two essential perfections — the Divine Justice and the Divine Veracity.

A necessity for punishing sin lies, it has been said, in the nature of sin itself, as deserving of punishment; punishment is *due* to sin ;—so that Justice has no place if punishment be set aside. But, is this indeed so? Punishment is *due* to sin, if *due* and *desert* be the same? Sin deserves punishment; and if Justice is wanting wherever there is not treatment according to desert, forbearing to punish is being unjust; and there is truly a hindrance to the remission of punishment still remaining in the Nature of God: He would be the author of injustice if He should forbear to punish. The high and unchangeable necessity of which we have again and again spoken, would be against admitting any substitute for the punishment of sin. No atonement is admissible, not even though the atonement be itself punishment, i. e., the punishment of another: for the argument is, that there must be punishment *where* and *because* it is deserved; and the sinner's desert of punishment is one of the things which are eternal.

10. But let it be inquired into, whether that is the true idea of Justice which leads to this conclusion? Is it so, that Justice implies and necessitates *treatment according to desert*, so that where there is sin there must be punishment, or Justice is sacrificed? The necessity of treatment according to desert—is this embraced in the nature of Justice? Is there, then, no such thing with God, as the remission of the punishment of sin, or veritable forgiveness? What means the preaching of the remission of sins among all nations in the name of Christ?*

Besides, how, after adopting this idea of Justice, can we give it a place among the Virtues? If Justice be a virtue, a good thing, it can never be opposed to any other virtue, or oblige us to anything evil, or be inconsistent with universal goodness. The Virtues are homogeneal, sisters in the same family; they love and embrace one another. If I must renounce Virtue—be malignant or vindictive, for example, in order to retain what I choose to call Justice, either Justice is now an evil thing, or I have abused it, by giving its name to that which is evil. That cannot be in its own nature good which requires us to be, or to do, evil. But suppose a man to be brought into judgment

* Luke xxiv. 47.

and condemned as a criminal; and that, by some means, the ends to be answered by his punishment are already secured — that through a certain arrangement or provision, no injury will be sustained, and no good be lost—no ill consequences of any kind will follow, by forbearing to punish him—so that if his punishment should take place it would be for no end but simply for punishment's sake ; and now suppose again, that something naming itself Justice should forbid his discharge on the ground that it would keep him from his desert, would this something, bear whatever name it may, be anything else than simple malignity—would it do in this case what might be regarded as a praiseworthy office, a thing worthy to be classed with the exercises and acts of that holy Love, which is the fulfilling of the moral law ? Surely it ought not to be called Justice. Is the quality of Justice such that it must inflict punishment, in all cases where it is merited, irrespectively of the ends of punishment, or merely because punishment has been incurred and is deserved? The ends of punishment must be regarded ; they are the justification and defence of its infliction—what Justice points to, it may be with tears of pity, as the necessitating cause of her severity. If these can be secured without punishment, it is not Justice, or any form of goodness, but arbitrary cruelty, that will proceed, in these circumstances, to inflict a pang, though death itself be *deserved*. Justice is in this case *satisfied*—she does not and cannot object to the remission of punishment: Justice is no enemy to Love.

11. It may be well to note the office and place of Justice in a Virtuous character. It is essential, but it does not hold the highest seat among the attributes of goodness. The supremacy belongs to Love — the highest, brightest adornment and glory of every good being. Wisdom is in the service of Love; so is Power; so is Justice. The work of Justice is to secure to all their rights, and protect the interests of all. This done, Justice is content; she seeks nothing more. If by any proceeding of Wisdom—any means whatever not unlawful in themselves—the interests of all are placed in perfect security, nothing would be more unjust and absurd than to forbid, in the name of Justice, the manifestations of mercy.

12. Distinctions have been made in Justice, as if it were of different kinds, *Distributive*, *Commutative*, and *Public;* but Justice in each of these varieties is of the same nature; in neither of them does it ever fulfil the part of simple despotic power, or renounce the rule of Love and Goodness. Distributive Justice deals out to every one the portion of good " which falleth to him;" allots to each one his claims, suffers no one to be injured; but it hinders no one from relinquishing his rights at the suggestion of benevolence or compassion, much less does it oblige any one to be malignant or unforgiving. Commutative Justice— faithfulness to contracts, honesty between man and man—is not against indulgence to an unfortunate debtor, nor will it imprison an honest debtor who has no means of payment; such a measure never proceeds from any modification of Justice; it is the doing of

pure malevolence. Public Justice is of the same character: it demands the punishment of crimes, as a means of securing the public good, but it is not against the pardon of an offender whose punishment may be remitted with prudence; or, as the case sometimes is, must be remitted, unless the public good be disregarded. To return to our former statement, it is never of the nature or spirit of Justice to give pain where no ulterior end is to be answered, where there is no object to be reached beyond the giving of pain, or where the infliction terminates in itself. Such severity proceeds not from Justice, but gratuitous cruelty. Justice, then, is not in the way.

13. The other supposed obstacle is the Divine Veracity. Punishment, we are reminded, is not only deserved, it is *threatened* and *denounced*. It is expressed in the Law itself, as the consequence of transgression, and is not the Law the voice of truth? Or is it consistent with the principle and end of Divine legislation, to allow the idea that what the Law names as the penalty of transgression, may be incurred and yet not endured? If this be so, is not the discouragement of transgression, the majesty of the Law—the strength of the Divine government, less than it might be?

It must be confessed that there is, on this supposition, less of one kind of strength than in the opposite view there would be. If the Divine government proceeded on the principle, adopted, it is said, by an ancient tyrant, that no remission or mitigation of the punishment prescribed in the law would, *under any circumstances*, be admitted, there would, indeed, be in it more of that terrible strength which is displayed in the stern exercise of authority; more, in other words, of despotic power. But it is impossible that God, a Being of perfect and unchangeable goodness, should administer such a government. He would not be God if He should assume the throne of an arbitrary despot. Any plan of government, not consistent with the supreme rule of Love or Goodness, is such as would dishonor the Most High. He could govern on no such plan. *If the remission of punishment may be made compatible with Justice,* it is reproachful to Him to suppose that He would, by institutes of law and government, have foreclosed against Himself the exercise of the pardoning prerogative; or disabled Himself from appearing in His administration true to His own nature as the God of Love, whose goodness is His glory.

The fact is, that mere legislation, unless it be itself unlawful, never binds the hands of love, or forbids mercy under all possible or supposeable circumstances. The veracity of a lawgiver is not pledged by the simple fact that he has annexed a penalty to his law, for the execution of the penalty in all cases of transgression. Let Justice be satisfied, and truth itself would lose the quality of a virtue, if it should now be a barrier to the free exercises of benevolence. Just legislation, like Justice itself, implies no necessity for punishment, except as the ends of punishment may require. The penalty of a law is "not to be taken for a prediction, expressive of a certain event, or what shall be; but a commination, expressing what is deserved, or most justly may be; the true meaning or design of a commination being, that it may never be executed."* They who think otherwise, "labor under a delusion as to the meaning of threatenings, which, though they affirm simply, nevertheless contain in them a tacit condition, depending on the result."† Such universally is the groundwork, the law, of all true legislation, human and Divine. Where law under the Divine government is broken, the penalty is incurred, the transgressor is amenable to punishment; but God has not, by the mere fact of having given the law, pronounced *a priori* against the exercise of mercy. He holds, and from the first meant to hold, the pardoning prerogative in His hand. Although, according to the letter of the law, the offender is exposed to death, yet God, except as justice demands satisfaction, has left Himself free to do with him as He pleases—to have mercy on whom He will have mercy, and show compassion to whom He will show compassion.

14. These Divine perfections, then, are not in the way. So far as Justice and Truth are concerned, the way is open and clear. Is there any other obstruction? If an amende, an atonement, may be supplied, is there anything remaining, in or out of the Divine nature, to restrain the exercise and manifestation of Divine benevolence to mankind?

According to the evangelical faith, such a measure has become a reality. An Atonement has been made, by means of which all the perfections of God harmonize and interblend their glories in favor of men; His

---

* Howe. † Calvin.

Justice, Truth, Holiness, Wisdom, commingling with His Mercy, and all perfectly consenting together, to set before us, as a free and sovereign gift, eternal life, with all its variety of infinite blessings. It is, we hold, a historical verity, that such a measure has come into existence and operation; has taken effect, and is the groundwork of the Divine dispensations of grace and goodness which so abound towards our sinful world. We regard it as the chief of all the ways of God— the foundation of His kingdom. The immediate agent by whom it was accomplished, was He to whom the Scripture refers, under the title, "the Captain of our salvation." The means were included in those sufferings of His, by which, as the Scripture saith, "He was made perfect." In these sufferings the Atonement is to be found. The Gospel of Jesus Christ records the history of the transaction. It had its consummation in the agony and bloody sweat and unparalleled death of Christ. "The decease which He accomplished at Jerusalem," including its preliminary and attendant particulars, *was an atonement*, a satisfaction to Divine Justice, whereby the door of salvation was opened to mankind. This is the grand article of evangelical Theology.

15. The doctrine embraces an *explanation*, showing why it was that this death had the efficacy which is ascribed to it; or what gave it its power to atone for sin. This arose in part from the nature of the death or sufferings of Christ; but chiefly from the character which the doctrine ascribes to the Sufferer. In this latter respect, the doctrine, without controversy, pre-

sents a great mystery. It gives to the Sufferer a sphere of antecedent and independent existence, out of and above the creation. It makes Him distinct from God,* and at the same time co-equal and co-eternal with Him; partaking with Him the essence and inherent glory of the Godhead :† whereby He was competent to dispose of Himself as He pleased, and also to suffer or do whatever might be exacted of Him for the satisfaction of Justice, without being Himself overcome and swallowed up, in meeting His dread liability. It affirms of Him, moreover, that He sustained a mysterious relation to God, that, namely, of an Only Begotten Son, who dwelt from eternity in the bosom of the Father. It adds, that this uncreated and co-eternal Companion and Son of God, came into the world, in the fulness of time, clothed in humanity, yet without sin, for the suffering of the death which awaited Him. Further, it represents Him as bearing, by the imputation of Justice, the sin of mankind; thus making His sufferings vicarious, while it gives them a severity not to be explained or justified under any other idea than that they were a substitute for our punishment—a compensation for its remission. Finally, it declares that by virtue of these sufferings, on the part of one who possessed the Divine nature in full equality with God, an Atonement was made—every end answered which could have been gained by inflicting condign punishment on mankind.

16. The sufficiency of this measure—its power to atone—no one, of course, could perfectly appreciate,

* " The Word was *with* God." † " The Word *was* God."

besides God Himself. None else could comprehend the amount of the guilt to be forgiven, or the punishment which it incurred; nor could any other estimate justly the value of the sufferings which were endured by Christ—such sufferings of such a personage. Their compensative merit, in their breadth and length, their depth and height, who but God alone could comprehend? But they must have been an adequate compensation, having been appointed and accepted as such by the Divine Justice: and now, since by the will of God they have been published and set forth as sufficient for their great purpose, that it has this sufficiency, or is a full amende or satisfaction to justice, cannot but assert itself in the consciousness of every one to whom it comes, in its just statement and influence. Being an atonement in fact, according to the judgment and testimony of God, it must be one in their experience. Having satisfied the ethical nature of God, it cannot but also satisfy conscience, or the ethical nature of man. The facts embraced in it,—that the sufferer was, in essential dignity, equal with God, and was also His Only Begotten Son, cannot but be regarded and accepted as constituting it an atonement. Let it be admitted, that the degraded man, whose sweat in the garden was as great drops of blood falling down to the ground, and who died on the cross in the manner described in the gospel, was the equal, and express image of God, the brightness of His glory, and His own Son; and that He suffered thus " to purge our sins," or make satisfaction for us to Justice; and though no finite mind can conceive the magnitude of the punishment due to mankind, yet sure and self-evident it is, that neither this punishment nor anything else, could have been of greater avail as expressive of the demerit of sin, and the Divine indignation towards it. Let the statement be apprehended and received by the human conscience, and it cannot but give that conscience peace and quietness, as to the *atoning sufficiency* of the stupendous Measure.*

17. But is the statement itself credible? Does it not involve intrinsic absurdity, or what is repugnant to reason and natural religion? Is not the possibility of an atonement grounded in an assertion respecting the character of Christ, which cannot be true? There could have been no atonement, it is said, if there had not been One in eternity with God, who Himself possessed the Divine attributes: in other words, it is taught, that Christ was strictly a Divine Person. This is the foundation of the doctrine of the atonement. Is it consistent with the greatest and first of all truths—the Unity of God? The statement is presented with a concession—rather with a bold

---

* It is sometimes said, that the identical penalty denounced against transgressors of the law was suffered by Christ; but that what Christ suffered, as to the matter of it, was not their penalty is certain: Edwards has indicated the difference in the following particulars:

1. Christ felt not the gnawings of a guilty condemning conscience.
2. He felt no torment from the reigning of inward corruption and lusts, as the damned do.
3. Christ had not to consider that God hated him.
4. Christ did not suffer despair, as the wicked do in hell.

Edwards' Works, vol. viii., p. 176. Dwight's edition.

averment, that it is in this respect a mystery; but it is a mystery and no more; it is not against any dictate of reason, or contradictory of the Divine Unity. In asserting the pre-existent and eternal Divinity of Christ, it does not deny the one and simple essence of God, but only implies that this one essence is *pluri-personal;* or that in the essence of the Deity there are more Persons or subsistences than one. There is nothing in reason, nothing in nature against this assertion. It relates to the mode of the Divine existence—a great mystery indeed. But to men, what is there that is not in some respect mysterious; and if all nature be full of mystery, why should we expect to find out by searching, the mode in which the great Infinite Himself subsists? The mystery, in this case, is one which, it is contended, the Scriptures reveal in a thousand places; which, indeed, including its cognate doctrines, is the subject-matter of the Bible. The only question is, Is the Bible understood and interpreted aright?

III.

NATURE OF THE ATONEMENT—II.

To this brief view of the Atonement, though we have endeavored to make it definite and distinctive, it may be proper to subjoin a few additional observations in order to insure it, if possible, against misapprehension.

1. The doctrine as now set forth, does not present God as divided against Himself, or the Persons of the Godhead as divided and contrary to one another; does not ascribe compassion to the Son and deny it to the Father. The whole Deity is made the Author and Finisher of the Atonement; the will and purpose of the entire Godhead were fulfilled; it was as much the doing of the Father as of the Son; the Son, while He gave Himself, was also the Father's gift. The conception of opposite feelings and interests is not justified, but precluded.

2. There is no ground for the objection, that it makes God *unjust* in order to be just,—unjust in His treatment of Christ, in order to be just in showing favor to the guilty. Christ does not become a sinner,

because by imputation He bears our sins. He is not regarded as deserving the treatment He receives. He is not treated otherwise than as He chooses to be. He simply foregoes His own honors and rights for a time, and offers Himself to suffer, as the necessary means of our salvation. He is not *punished*, in the ordinary meaning of the word, as implying personal criminality. No injustice is done Him, unless it be in the nature of Justice to permit no sacrifice to be made, no interest or right surrendered for the benefit of others; unless Justice be the enemy of self-denial and disinterested benevolence.

3. The Atonement does not imply that there is a vindictive propensity in the Divine nature; or that God needs compensative sufferings for His own gratification, or any motives out of Himself in order to be inclined to the exercise of compassion. It supposes the Deity to be incapable of acting with impropriety, or in a manner which does not become Him, but not to be vindictive or slow to mercy. The Atonement assumes as a necessity, that every Divine attribute harmonize in every Divine act or proceding; and that the Divine conduct can never be out of keeping with itself, or inconsistent with the majesty and honor of God, as the Lord and Maker of all. But this is not against the purest and highest benevolence; it is only against a benevolence falsely so called, which, by disregarding mode in manifesting itself, would defeat all the ends of Infinite goodness. The Atonement is but the mercy or goodness of God, using a proper mode of showing itself to man. Instead of being against

goodness, it is an instance of goodness, comprehending every other, and also infinitely surpassing all other forms of goodness possible or conceivable. It is the chief means by which God demonstrates His goodness.

There are representations in evangelical writings and discourses which, taken to the letter, and apart from their connexions, are to the discredit of the Atonement, as implicating the Divine character in reproach. The Atonement is said to be the appeasement of the Divine vengeance; the wrath of God is set forth as spending and exhausting itself on the pure and innocent Saviour, etc. But these are bold and strong expressions, the import of which, as consisting with just views of the Divine goodness, is commonly obvious from their context and scope. They are not without warrant from Scripture.* They make no bad impression on candid minds. When it is kept in mind that the Atonement is God's own work, that Christ was His own Son, in whom He was always well pleased, and that His treatment of Christ was, in fact, a sacrifice infinitely expensive to Himself, no room is left for understanding the language in question as imputing malignant feelings to the Deity. It serves but to show the malignant nature of sin, and the greatness of the love of God to man.†

---

* Zech. xiii. 7. Is. liii. 10. Rom. iii. 25.

† It is a theological question, whether Avenging or punitive justice is natural to God. (*An justitia vindicatrix naturalis sit Deo.*) If Justice be taken as we have presented it, the question must be answered in the affirmative, even if we understand the words, "natural to God," as implying that God would lose His true nature or be no longer God, if He should be without

4. It is not true of the Atonement* that it is incomprehensible or obscure as to the manner in which it answers its end. Nothing in the Atonement is more manifest than its mode of influence, or *how* it is connected with forgiveness and salvation. An attempt to state the doctrine, which does not show this connection, omits the radical idea of the Atonement. The Atonement, in its very definition, declares *how* it opens the door for the manifestations of mercy. What is the Atonement but a satisfaction to Justice, as complete as would have been our punishment, in order to the remission of punishment without dishonor to God, and without detriment to His law and government? And is it still a mystery *how* the Atonement is connected with our salvation? There is mystery in some things pertaining to the Atonement, but it is denying the doctrine to say that we know nothing of the mode of its influence.

5. The Atonement cannot with propriety be regarded as a *strictly forensic* transaction. Where the terms peculiar to courts of judicature are used in speaking of it, they are not to be taken literally; but, as human language must needs be taken very

---

avenging justice; that is to say, if He did not execute punishment at the behest of love. This justice is indeed *natural* to God; and the very strong authropopathic language referred to in the text, and examples of the Divine severity in punishment, may be cited in proof of the assertion. But if we take Avenging Justice in a sense which allows a disconnection of it from the rule of love, and suppose its inflictions to be for their own sake, merely, and ascribe it to the nature of God, we make Him an object of horror.

* As Mr. Coleridge, Dr. Paley and others say.

often when used to express Divine things, with more or less accommodation to the nature of the subject, as by its own evidence, or by other means, understood. The Atonement, for example, *justifies* no one in the forensic sense, the satisfaction which it makes not being such as the law exacts from debtors or criminals. Forensic justification and satisfaction are incompatible with forgiveness: he who is justified in a court cannot be pardoned: he whose debt is discharged cannot be forgiven: but the Atonement does not render our free and gratuitous forgiveness an impossibility. Its influence is precisely the reverse; namely, to make our forgiveness consistent with the perfection and glory of God; or if we may so speak, to obtain the consent of Justice and all the other Divine attributes to the exercise of the pardoning power. The Atonement does not give us a claim on God, on the ground of justice; it does not impose a necessity or obligation on God to forgive us; it does not deprive Him of His high prerogative, as Judge and Lord of all, to have mercy on whom He will have mercy: it does not transfer this prerogative from Himself to Christ, or give it to the Son exclusively of the Father. We have mentioned what it does. It brings all the perfections of God into harmony with the free manifestations of His mercy; so that in making these manifestations He acts as " becomes Him for whom are all things and by whom are all things."

6. There is a theory of the Atonement which makes the believer's discharge from punishment a matter of debt to him from God. It supposes him, on his be-

coming a believer, or accepting the Atonement, unamenable to punishment on the score of distributive justice, square with the law, its demands against him having been fully met by his Surety, in such a sense, that to punish him would be injustice to him, a double infliction of the very punishment he had incurred. It limits grace in our salvation to providing the Atonement; that was an affair of grace; all after that was debt, absolute debt to the believer. It expresses itself on this point in the following emphatic language: "The Justice of God that required man's damnation, and seemed inconsistent with his salvation, now does as much require the salvation of those that believe, as ever before it required their damnation. Salvation is an absolute debt to the believer from God, so that he may in justice challenge and demand it; not upon the account of what he himself has done, but upon the account of what his Surety has done. For Christ has satisfied justice fully for his sin; so that it is a thing that may be challenged, that God should release the believer from punishment; it is but a piece of justice that the creditor should release the debtor, when he has fully paid the debt." Nor is this the full extent of his demand on Divine justice: "The believer may demand *eternal life*, because it has been merited by Christ by *a merit of condignity*, so that it is contrived that that Justice that seemed to require man's destruction, now requires his salvation."* Is this the teachings of the Bible?

* This citation is from President Edwards. Professor Park remarks concerning it, (Theory of Atonement,) that it was written

The Bible teaches the doctrine of *forgiveness of sins*, as well as Atonement, *through the grace of God*. Discriminating (Eph. iv. 33,) between Christ and God who, though the same in one respect are not so in another, it declares that GOD *forgives us*,—forbears to treat us as we deserve, not pays us what is, in justice, due to us from Him,—*for Christ's sake*, or on account of the Atonement which he made. It is impossible to imagine a greater contrast than that of the doctrine of the Bible and the doctrine of this theory, in regard to the claim of believers for their salvation. The opposite of the latter doctrine it could not have asserted if it has not done so. Instead of making the Atonement inconsistent with forgiveness, it makes forgiveness—free forgiveness by the grace of God,—the very object and fruit of the Atonement. Instead of limiting grace to providing the Atonement, it makes it the very function of that stupendous work of grace, to remove obstacles to the farther manifestations of grace. Instead of leaving no place for the exercise of grace after the first office of it—or having mercy on whom He will have mercy, a prerogative of God no longer, it assigns to the Atonement the virtue of enabling Him, if we may speak thus, to exercise this prerogative consistently with Justice. Instead of empowering believers to demand salvation as a debt due to them from Him, it summons all men to lift up prayer to Him for pardon and daily bread, and whatsoever else of good they would receive from Him. It sets forth

by Edwards " when he was only thirty years old, and was pointedly condemned by Dr. Smalley."

God[*] in absolute independence of all creatures as to claims on His favor ; and in respect to sinners, while it announces Him as appeased or propitiated toward them, by virtue of the Atonement, it still leaves them at the disposal of His mercy, which on their acceptance of the Atonement, He is more than willing for Christ's sake to extend to them ; but to the Atonement itself, infinitely precious as it is in His sight, it ascribes no influence restrictive of freedom in dispensing mercy, whether in making sinners "willing" in the day of his power to accept his grace, or in realizing to them its fulness, afterwards. It reveals God as a Promiser, it is true, and lays the utmost stress on the divine benignity as shown in the freeness and abundance of His promises ; and pleads with us by the argument that God cannot fail to keep His word to the uttermost ; it allows us—strange to think—to hold Him to His word, to prove Him, to test His fidelity ; but both in promising and keeping His promise, it is not justice to them but pure love that actuates Him, and such love as only the infinitude of His own nature could express or contain.

7. The theory of the Atonement, therefore, which gives it a virtue to render God a debtor to believers, is not the true theory. There is no such virtue in the Atonement. Creatures, not to say sinners, cannot be put into relations toward God, which would make a claim on Him, in justice, either proper to them as dependent on Him, not only for what of good or goodness they may have, but even for existence ; or, consistent

[*] Rom. xi. 25.

with the absolute and indefeasible independence of the Deity as the sole Original Fountain of created good and being. There is no possibility of adding to the merit of the Atonement. Among the works of God, there is nothing so worthy of praise as what our Blessed Lord achieved, when uttering on the Cross the words, *It is finished*, he bowed his head in the death of propitiation. Nothing has received such expressions of complacency from God, such Alleluias from the hosts of heaven: Nothing has been, nothing, in all ages to come, is to be so rewarded. But for some purposes, nevertheless, it has no competence; and one of these is, to entitle men to demand their salvation as an absolute debt to them from God. And it is not lessening its value to deny that it has a competency for this; nay, it would take away all value from it to give it this competency: it would then become a greater power for evil, than it now is for good. If it might in some sense save men, it might dethrone and undeify God.

8. The theory mistakes in thinking to bring the idea of *condignity* into the rationale of the Atonement. There is no such thing as Creature-merit, as pertaining to God. It is alike *impossible* and *unnecessary*. First, it is impossible: Creatures may have claims on one another. The laborer is worthy of his hire: but while His creatures are indebted to God for every thing, He can owe them nothing. "For who hath first given to Him and it shall be recompensed unto him again?" Even Christ, when He became a man and so entered into the relations

of the finite, could not in these relations make God a debtor. It became Him, it was what He owed Himself as well as God, to fulfil all righteousness. It was otherwise before He became a man, or while He remained in the sphere of pure Godhead. But when He became human, it behooved Him to meet the conditions of that nature. He bound Himself thereby to absolute obedience to God, and did no more than it became Him to do. His putting Himself into human relations, which He was infinitely above all obligations to do, together with His subsequent obedience unto death, gave His work an excellence not to be measured by finite thought; but even this could not lay God under the obligations of a debtor: God who alone could appreciate such excellence, could not but have an infinite complacency in it; but He was not bound except as by His own engagement He bound Himself, to save mankind for the sake of it. And as this kind of merit was impossible, so, as we have said, it was also *unnecessary.* God did not require a merit of *condignity*, to make him favorable to us: all He required was, that the obstacles to the exercise of His love, which our sin put in its way, be removed; after that His love needed no motive but itself; it had motive enough in its nature: love seeketh not her own; she is moved for others' good: her *nature* impels her, and when once her way is prepared, there is nothing she will not do to give herself a complete development—to multiply favor, until it would be favor no longer to do so.

9. We have thus seen that there cannot and need

not be a meriting of salvation; but we must say more than this; the *desert* of punishment cannot be taken away. The Atonement can do no more than cover the guilt of man, that is to say, secure him against punishment; it cannot make him innocent. The wages of sin are still his due, his only due; they need not be given him, but he deserves, in justice, nothing else. Upon his becoming a believer, God for Christ's sake remits his punishment, adopts him, takes him into highest favor, treats him, as if, to use the language of Paul,* he had become "the righteousness of God;" but in all this he is still undeserving, and God does but exercise mercy; sovereign and boundless mercy. So it is, and it is impossible it should be otherwise. Ill-desert once contracted, the fact remains forever, and its nature is also eternal.

10. The theory, therefore, of the Atonement, which makes this, the greatest of the works of infinite wisdom and love, a payment of a debt, putting believers in a relation to law,† by which they require a right to salvation as a debt due to them from God, is not the true one. We accept no theory as a full explanation of the subject. We are persuaded that its philosophy is completely comprehended only by the mind of the Infinite. Its idea,

* 2 Cor., v. 21.

† The theory, to make itself complete, applies most thoroughly its idea of the merit of condignity. Regarding the transgressor in his two-fold relation to the penalty and the precept of the law, it divides the work of Christ, so as to accommodate this view, into two parts; one his passive righteousness or sufferings and death, to meet the liability to the penalty; the other, his active righteousness or obedience to fulfil the precept. By the first, a discharge from punishment is merited, by the second, eternal life.

in its fullness, exists as it has done from eternity in that mind; doubtless it has never entered, and will never enter into any other. The more we consider the subject, the more we distrust all philosophizing on it, farther than to exclude inconsistency with known truth; which is all that we have attempted. The full significance of the facts of the Atonement, the incarnation, the temptation, the agony and bloody sweat, the desertion and outcry on the cross, the death and burial of Christ,—can neither be explained nor fully comprehended by man: neither can the teaching of Scripture concerning these facts. The language employed by the Bible in communicating this great lesson—"The Lord laid on him the iniquity of us all," "Awake, O sword, against the man that is my fellow," "He was made a curse for us," "He who knew no sin was made sin for us," "Through the eternal Spirit he offered himself without spot unto God," "By himself he purged our sins," "He was the propitiation for our sins," etc., can never be adequately rendered into logical definitions or the statements of human systems. The more profoundly it is pondered, the more the mind strives to take in its full meaning, the more is its wonder; the more its amazement such as that expressed by the holy apostle in his exclamation, "O the depth!"—the more cold and sterile appear all human theories; the more suitable the prayer of À Kempis: "Let all teachers be silent, let the whole creation be dumb before Thee, and do Thou only speak to my soul."

11. The extent of the Atonement is determined from its nature. How far indeed it is to avail in actually

saving men, or to how many it is to be applied, or what portion of mankind were, as its fruit, destined to salvation by the eternal purpose of God, cannot be understood from the Atonement itself. The satisfaction which it renders for sin, not being like the payment of a debt, inconsistent with, but only the necessary condition of, forgiveness, the Atonement of itself involves the actual salvation of none. Certain indeed it was, that this Provision of infinite wisdom and goodness would not be without fruit; but to render the Atonement effectual, other agencies and influences, those especially of the renewing and sanctifying Spirit, must be employed. In respect to its application or success, the Atonement will be coincident in extent with that of the Divine purpose: But the Atonement *proper*, the Atonement in itself, or its efficacy *precisely as an Atonement*, has an amplitude and a sufficiency equal to the value of the blood of Christ—the infinite worth of His sufferings and death. The overture of salvation to man is limited in Scripture to no age, no country, no class, no number; it is made, not to as many as God secretly intends to make willing to accept it, but with the same earnestness to those who are not made willing; nothing limits it but incorrigible obstinacy of will in those by whom it is not received. The boundlessness of the overture has an adequate ground in the Atonement, whose breadth and length are also without bound.

12. Again, the Atonement is adapted to have influences and effects ulterior to the salvation of men. By the discoveries which it makes, the lessons of wis-

dom, justice, purity, power, and goodness which it inculcates, and the manner in which it enforces them, it is suited to be the teacher of the world and the ages—the great light, the central sun of the moral creation. The impression of necessities which it makes—the necessity that the ways of the Most High be always as becometh His essential majesty and glory; that order be preserved in the Divine kingdom; that the displeasure of God against sin be revealed; and the necessity of punishment, or else of satisfaction, in order to this revelation; and the other mysterious necessities which are shown in making satisfaction;—how fitted is an Expedient of this import and this power of enforcement, to uphold the universe in love and allegiance to Him, by whose infinite goodness it was devised and accomplished? That it is not hidden from any part of the creation, and that it is, in fact, the pillar and ground, the strength and security of the moral empire of the Almighty, the bond of eternal union and harmony among angels and men, and all the sons of light, is a scriptural asseveration concerning it, which has a high ground of probability in itself.

13. The distinguishing traits of evangelical piety appear in high relief in the light which shines from the Atonement. It is this doctrine which gives evangelical piety its peculiarity. That piety takes from the Atonement its entire image and fashion, its every line and point, as the clay receives whatever is engraved on the seal. The Atonement in evangelical doctrine is a fullness that filleth all in all. It is

the ground of all, it sustains all, it permeates all, it gives life and form and power to all. It has the same pre-eminence and importance in the piety which corresponds to this doctrine as its just counterpart. The impress of the Atonement on the soul and the character is the sum, the *all* of evangelical piety. That piety is nothing else than the doctrine of Christ, co-existent and co-eternal with God ; Deity incarnate, suffering for the sins of men, the Just instead of the unjust ;—this doctrine written on the heart by the Spirit of the Living God, and exhibited in the life and conduct. We have not time to examine this subjective image particularly—the sense of mystery and wonder, the humility, the annihilation of self-wisdom, self-righteousness, and self-will, the filial dread of the Divine majesty, the contrition and brokenness of heart, the sense of the evil of sin, the love and delight in Christ, the love and gratitude to God, the peace, the joy, the hope, the praise, and other traits comprised in it : But one thing we cannot forbear to observe: that there is in the piety which answers to the Atonement as the image to the seal, an absolute, overwhelming conviction of the final and aggravated condemnation of unbelievers. That the Atonement, with all its inherent evidences of divinity, and all the testimonial signs and wonders, and other outward proofs by which it is confirmed, should not be received by those to whom it is offered ; that this great salvation should be neglected, this only means be despised, by which man could be saved ; how appalling the thought of such desperate wickedness!

How shall they escape, where shall they appear, who, in the language of Scripture, "tread under foot the Son of God?"

There is a piety whose most distinguishing characteristic seems to be aversion to that which is termed Evangelical. It has many recommendations. It melts with tenderness, it bows with reverence, it smiles with complacency, it rejoices with confidence and hope, at its own religious views. It often discourses with fluent and gentle, and tasteful language, in praise of itself; and it certainly has many fruits of natural goodness and self-culture to boast of. But so inimical is it to the majesty and glory of God, that when the great Device is mentioned, by which alone it was made possible to keep the Divine honor unsullied and immaculate, while grace is shown to men, then this piety is ready to cry out, "away with it, away with it," as the Jews expressed their scorn for the Son of God, when Pilate brought him forth to them, saying, "behold your king." No wickedness moves its indignation sooner or more profoundly than the doctrine of the Atonement. If that doctrine be true, of what avail will this piety be, "when God taketh away the soul?"

IV.

CHRIST PRE-EXISTENT;

AS ASSERTED IN JOHN I. 1-5.

"*In the beginning was the Word, and the Word was with God, and the Word was God. The same was in the beginning with God. All things were made by Him; and without Him was not any thing made that was made. In Him was life; and the Life was the light of men. And the light shineth in darkness; and the darkness comprehended it not.*"

OUR familiarity with these words, unless it has rendered us unthinking, cannot have diminished our interest in them. Francis Junius, of whom, at his death, it was remarked by Scaliger, that the whole world lamented him as its instructor,[*] was recovered from atheism in a remarkable manner, by this passage of Scripture. Persuaded by his father to read the New Testament, "at first sight," he says, "I fell unexpectedly on that august chapter of St. John the Evangelist, 'In the beginning was the Word,' etc. I read

---

[*] Junius, and Joseph Scaliger were Professors at Leyden, at the same time. Scaliger had a strong aversion for Junius in his lifetime, because the latter took the liberty to contradict him sometimes in matters of chronology, and opposed his having the precedency over all the other professors. But at the death of Junius, the resentment of Scaliger gave place to the strongest feelings of respect which expressed themselves in an admirable panegyric.

part of the chapter, and was so struck with what I read, that I instantly perceived the divinity of the subject, and the authority and majesty of the Scripture, to surpass greatly all human eloquence. I shuddered in my body; my mind was confounded; and I was so strongly affected all that day, that I hardly knew who I myself was: but Thou, Lord my God, didst remember me in thy boundless mercy, and receive a lost sheep into thy flock."

What is the subject of these wonderful assertions? What is meant by the appellation, THE WORD, by which that subject is expressed?

In the first place, does it denote a Being, or an attribute; a Person, or a quality?

That a real Person was intended, should never, we think, have been questioned. It is affirmed that this Word was with God, was God,* created all things, was testified unto by John, was made flesh, and dwelt with men, full of grace and truth. There is an irreverent freedom, to suspect nothing worse, in that criticism which ventures to inquire whether the Evangelist meant anything more than an attribute or quality, that is, no real subsistence, by what he denominates the Word in this sublime passage. He does not more explicitly affirm the Personal existence and individu-

---

* "On this supposition," namely, that an attribute was intended, "the commencement of the Gospel, would be altogether tautological: 'In the beginning was the wisdom of God, this divine wisdom was with God, and God was this divine wisdom.' The Evangelist would have had no occasion to establish the identity of the Logos with God, if he had intended to denote by Logos, nothing else than a Divine attribute."—*Tholuck*.

ality of Jesus Christ, the subject of his Gospel, than the perfect Personality of the Word, the subject of his great declarations in this place.

Next, Who was the Individual intended by this appellation? We hesitate not to say that the evidence could not be more perfect than it is, that the self-same Person is here spoken of, whom the Evangelist afterwards presents in a human form, and under a human name, as the subject of his narrative. The Word here intended was our Lord Jesus Christ. To argue on this point, implies, in our view, a doubt whether the Evangelist did not mean to practice a deception on his readers.

But why, thirdly, does he give Christ this mysterious appellation? That some reason for this existed, we cannot but think. None of the names given to our Lord, were given arbitrarily. They were all chosen from their being significative of Him, in either his nature, or his office. What is there in the present appellation that renders it an appropriate name for our Lord Jesus Christ?

We think with Clarke, that this name should have been left untranslated. The original LOGOS is, he justly remarks, as proper an appellative of the Saviour of the world, as either of the terms JESUS or CHRIST. And as it would be improper to say, the Deliverer, the Anointed, instead of Jesus Christ, so it is improper to say, the Word, instead of the Logos.

It should be premised also, that this appellative had been used before the Evangelist wrote, with a deeply significant reference. Philosophers had used it to designate the creative power, to which in opposition to the doctrine of chance, they ascribed the origin of the Universe.* It was in use too among the Jewish teachers, who employed it to discriminate the Deity *revealed*, from the Deity *un-revealed*—a distinction which they seem to have derived from certain passages in the Old Testament; assisted, however, as Tholuck thinks, by the ancient oriental theosophy.† This fact accounts for the Evangelist's using the term as if it needed no explanation.‡ It was a term already in

---

* "The Platonists make mention of the Logos in this way:— καϑ' ον αει οντα, τα γενομενα εγενετο—by whom eternally existing all things were made."—*Clarke.*

† The passages from the Old Testament cited and commented on by Tholuck are Exod. xxxiii. 14. xx. 23. Is. lxiii. 9. Mal. iii. 1. Ps. xxxiii. 6. Prov. viii. 23 seq. These passages he shows, we think, contain the distinction; but he supposes it improbable that the Jewish teachers would have discovered it in them, but for their acquaintance with the oriental systems of religion. "In several of these systems, the idea that the highest Being is in himself incomprehensible and unapproachable, is found developed under various modifications. Man is represented as being seized with dizziness, when he attempts to comprehend this idea; and in general there is no transit from this Being to a world of created existences. Consequently it becomes necessary for God to generate in Himself a certain transition-point, to make His fulness comprehensible and communicable; and this He did by producing out of Himself from eternity, a Being like unto Himself through whom the concealed God was manifested."—The reader will find in *Smith's Scripture Testimony to the Messiah*, Vol. I. pp. 548—569, *third edition*, a collection of the principal passages in the extant writings of Philo, concerning the subject of the Logos. Philo was a Jew of Alexandria, of a sacerdotal family, who is supposed to have been about sixty years old at the death of Christ. His expressions concerning the Logos, have excited great admiration.

‡ "Since it can be actually proved, that the words ὁ λόγος τοῦ θεοῦ at that time expressed a definite doctrinal conception, and

familiar use, and used, unquestionably, to designate a Person. Mankind had been taught the doctrine of the Divine unity; they had also received some intimations of the doctrine of the Logos. Their knowledge on the latter subject, however, was extremely confused. The Evangelist has delivered concerning the Logos sublime and distinct statements, and identified the very Person to whom that name appropriately belongs. The true Logos, of whom the Old Testament had given some discoveries and promises, but of whom the philosophers and rabbis had ignorantly discoursed, was, the Evangelist here affirms, Jesus Christ, the Lord and Saviour of the world.*

such an one as is similar to that of John, it is altogether certain that John employed the Word in that determinate doctrinal sense which was prevalent in his time."—*Tholuck.*

* Tholuck rejects the idea that the Evangelist had allusion to the doctrine of the theosophists on this subject. "Since we find in the first place, that previously in the Old Testament, intimations of this doctrine of the Logos can be pointed out; and secondly, that the apostle Paul teaches the same doctrine of the Logos, Col. i. 15; 2 Cor. iv. 4; comp. Heb. i. 3, although he borrowed his mode of teaching neither from the Orientals nor from Philo, but from Jewish theologians only; and thirdly, since in Sir. xliii. 26 (28), the creative word of God, and in the book of Wisdom xviii. 15, the angel which presided over the theocracy of the Old Testament, is called λόγος; it must seem to be most probable that John did not occupy himself with the dogmas of other religions, but adhered to the Jewish doctrinal theology of his time, which was based on the Old Testament; and that in this way he made known that the Revealer of God pointed out in the Old Testament—He who had directed the administration of the Old Testament theocracy, had actually appeared in Christ. In the Epistles also, 1 John i. 1, and in the Revelation xix. 13, John calls Christ the Logos, and thereby intimates the important meaning of this appellation." As the Evangelist wrote, as

The propriety of giving Christ this appellation will, in some measure, appear by considering that He is, as Philo in speaking on the subject of the Logos, or *Word*, admirably says, THE SAME TO THE SUPREME INTELLECT, THAT SPEECH IS TO THE HUMAN. All who believe in the Scriptures admit that Christ is, in some sense, the REVEALER of God. The Scriptures teach nothing more explicitly than that the Deity, *except as revealed by Christ*, is at this day and forever will be hidden out of sight, and out of thought, to the entire universe of men and angels. That God "*could* not make an external revelation of Himself in the world until He had become revealed within Himself, that is, in the Son," is affirmed (how intelligibly different persons will differently decide) by the excellent expositor Tholuck; however this may be, it is the clear teaching of Scripture, that in point of fact, God, by Jesus Christ, has exerted all the power which He ever has exerted out of Himself, and made all the disclosures of Himself to creatures which ever have been made. That whatever knowledge men have of God and divine things, they have obtained through Christ, He Himself affirms: "No one hath seen God at any time; the only begotten Son who is in the bosom of the Father, He hath declared Him." It is related in the Old Testament that God was seen by Adam, Abraham, Moses and the prophets; but

---

he was moved by the Holy Ghost, he was competent to make known that the Revealer of God pointed out in the Old Testament had appeared in Christ, without being indebted to either the Jewish theologians of his time or the eastern theosophists.

they saw Him only in the Person of Christ, who also, by His Spirit, gave to holy men of old "the lively oracles" of inspired truth. Now, as speech is the medium by which knowledge is communicated among ourselves, it is manifestly proper that the source and channel of all true knowledge should, in a revelation given to man, be denominated the Logos—a term which signifies speech, or instruction, or the word spoken, or, as in our translation, the Word. There is, doubtless, more of fitness in this appellation to the Person to whom it is given than we can understand, but it is sufficiently obvious, that while there is mystery, there is also intelligible and striking propriety in naming our Lord the Logos.

Having seen that the term, in its present use, designates a Person, and that this Person was Christ, let us proceed to consider the announcements concerning him, which follow:

I. The first is, that Christ was in existence at the birth of the creation. The phrase "In the beginning"—the same with which Moses commences the Bible, refers us to the date of the creation, there being nothing to limit or qualify it. The assertion is that the Logos was in the beginning; the question may be asked, in the beginning of what? of the world as it now is? of the dealings of God with man? of the Christian dispensation? And men may give their own answers. The Evangelist is silent. He leaves us with the unqualified affirmation that the Logos was in the beginning—an affirmation which, if taken in the absolute sense, transfers us to the instant when creation had its origin and time with it, and presents to us Christ as then in existence.

The assertion here is, unless it should be understood with some restriction of which the Evangelist gives no hint, that Christ was in existence at the creation of the world; that when there were no depths—when there were no fountains abounding with water—before the mountains were settled—before the hills—while as yet God had not made the earth, nor the fields, nor the highest part of the dust of the world—when He prepared the heavens—when He set a compass upon the face of the depth—when He established the clouds above—when he strengthened the fountains of the deep—when He gave to the sea his decree that the waters should not pass his commandment—when He appointed the foundations of the earth*—then existed our Saviour Jesus Christ.

There are those, however, who restrict the words before us, so as to make them mean, *in the beginning of the preaching of the gospel*. It is not probable that many readers of the Evangelist will adopt this gratuitous exposition. It gives a trivial sense to one of the most remarkable texts of inspiration, and thus subjects itself to contempt.†

* In this use of Prov. viii. 22–30, to express what we believe to be asserted by the Evangelist as an historical fact, we design not to cite it as a parallel passage. It was, however, understood by the Jews of old, and the Christian church from the beginning, of a *Person*, the *substantial wisdom* of God; and whatever advances have been made in the science of interpretation, we question the soundness of that criticism which takes it in a different sense. See Waterland's Eight Sermons, pp. 216–218.

† Tholuck calls it the *shallow* Socinian explanation.

This assertion stands and ever will stand, without limitation or addition.

But taking it thus, what is it that it requires us to believe concerning Jesus Christ? That He is a Being, in the strictest sense, eternal! If He was in existence when the world and time commenced, He did not Himself then come into existence. To make Him one of the objects that then came into existence, to say that in the beginning He began to be, or that among those existences which came forth out of nothing at the command of the Creator, was the Logos, is to contradict the assertion that He was already in existence when the beginning took place. Well have the ancient Fathers said that "He who was in the beginning comprehended every beginning in himself,"* and that "as to the Being who was from the beginning, no time can be found when He was not."† It is therefore the proper import of the words of the Evangelist, that the attribute of eternity, in the most perfect sense, belongs to Christ; that as the prophet Micah affirms of Him, His emanations are from the beginning, from the days of eternity.

II. We are next informed, that Christ in eternity was the *Companion* of God. This is asserted not once only, but to give it stronger impression it is repeated in the second verse. *The same was in the beginning with God.* Eternal accompanying with Eternal! An unsearchable mystery, but yet a fact, to which the highest importance is attached in the Scriptures. In the statements of Scripture, concerning both crea-

---

* Augustine.   † Theophylact.

tion and redemption, the proposition that God did not dwell alone in that eternity which anteceded both, that the Logos was with Him there, is always implied and is often prominent. We do not give it as the assertion of the Scriptures, though a great commentator has made it, that God could not, except through the Son, have made an external revelation of Himself in the world; but that in point of fact He has not any otherwise revealed Himself in the world, that before creation was entered upon, there was, to speak after the manner of men, a consultation held, and an arrangement agreed upon, between God and the Logos, and that both creation and redemption were the fruit not of God's agency apart from that of the Logos, but of the concurrence and intercommunion of both; and further, that but for the part agreed to be fulfilled, and in due time actually fulfilled, by the Logos, there never would have been either redemption or creation—is not only a statement, but the leading and fundamental statement of the Bible. That book does not speak concerning the origin and authorship of the universe, as too many do who profess to take it as the standard of their faith. It tells of a creating Deity, but it also tells of one inhabiting, with that Deity, the eternity which preceded creation, and equally concerned in accomplishing that glorious work: "The Lord possessed me in the beginning of His way, before His work of old. I was set up from everlasting, from the beginning, or ever the earth was: Then I was by Him as one brought up with Him; and I was daily His delight, rejoicing always before Him—rejoicing in the habitable part of His earth, and my delights were with sons of men."* The Bible teaches that the universe was created *for* Christ, and with reference to a revelation of the divine glory to be made by Christ, through the instrumentality of various redemptive and governmental agencies; and that redemption itself, except through Christ, was not achievable without a sacrifice of the Divine Justice. From which clearly stated premises the conclusion is, that had there been no Christ, no Logos, in eternity, there had been no world, no creation, no time. We are accustomed in our devout meditations to trace our salvation to a covenant or agreement entered into, in eternity, between the Father and the Son, and to admit that but for what the Son then consented to do for us, our salvation would have been unaccomplished; but the Bible leads us to take a wider survey, and to see in the existence and agency of the Logos, the foundation of the existence and perpetuity of all creatures and worlds. The doctrine of a Personal Logos, the Companion of God in eternity, enters as distinctly into the biblical system of the universe, as the doctrine of a Divine existence; and the great Lord Bacon has shown himself as sound in the faith, as he was in philosophy, in that memorable confession of his, from which we give the

---

* This language is not introduced as proof, but as happily suited to express the sense intended to be conveyed by the author. That it is, however, applicable to Christ in the strictest sense, was the universal opinion of the ancients (themselves, be it remembered, *Orientals* and therefore), perhaps the best qualified to give the true exposition.

following extract: "That neither angels, man, nor world, would stand, or can stand one moment in God's eye, without His beholding the same IN THE FACE OF A MEDIATOR; and therefore that before Him with whom all things are present, *the Lamb of God* was slain before all worlds; but that out of His eternal and infinite goodness and love, purposing to become a Creator, and to communicate to His creatures, He ordained in His eternal counsel, that one Person of the Godhead should be united to one nature and to one particular of His creatures; so that in the Person of the Mediator the true ladder may be fixed whereby God may descend to His creatures, and His creatures might ascend to God; so that God, by the reconcilement* of the Mediator, turning His countenance toward His creatures, (though not in equal light and degree) made way unto the dispensation of His most holy and sacred will; whereby some of His creatures might stand

---

* Lord Bacon, on the basis of such scriptures as Job iv. 18; Job xxv. 5; Isa. xxiv. 23, and of his own exquisite sense of what is fit and seemly, held that the reason or ground of necessity for a Mediator was the ineffable purity and majesty of God. The writer once questioned if it be consistent with the infinite goodness of the Deity to suppose that He would not converse with innocent and pure creatures except through a mediator. Reflection has convinced him that Lord Bacon is sustained in his belief by both Scripture and reason. It may be the highest goodness to inspire even unfallen creatures with a sense of infinite majesty and greatness; the want of that sense might be the means of their ruin; and in order to produce it in them, Mediation might have been indispensable. God is too good not to express delight in upright creatures, but it might have been unwise and contrary to goodness to be regardless of the mode in which His delights should be manifested.

and keep their state; others might possibly fall and be restored; and others might fall and not be restored to their estate, but yet remain in being though under wrath and corruption; *all with respect to the Mediator*, which is the great mystery and perfect centre of all God's ways with His creatures, and to which all his other works and wonders, do but serve and refer." That doctrine of the Logos, which makes Him the Companion, in eternity, of the eternal God, was, in the belief of Lord Bacon, as it is in the explicit testimony of Scripture, the foundation-stone of the systems of creation and redemption.

III. The next of the anouncements before us is that Christ, the Companion of God in eternity, was also God Himself. THE LOGOS WAS GOD. This is not a more explicit assertion of the Deity of Christ, than the phrase of which it is the translation. The translation is literally exact. This no criticism questions; but still there is a criticism which will not take this as a proof-text of the strict Deity of Christ. It asserts that he was God, but " if we suppose the word Logos to mean the reason, or wisdom, or power of God, what can that reason, or wisdom or power be, but God?"*
The evidence however that the word Logos, means not an attribute but a Person, is as we have before

---

* " A man's word, or thought, is not called *man ;* nor would the word, or wisdom of God be called *God*, if a mere attribute, or operation only was intended, and not a real person."—*Waterland.* That a prosopopoeia cannot be here admitted, is further evident from the fact, that it would, as Tholuck has remarked, render the expression tautological : " *The wisdom of God, personified, was God !*"

remarked such, that it requires a degree of opinionativeness not often found, capable of offering it resistance. Recourse therefore has been had to another supposition, namely, that an inferior and subordinate godship is here ascribed to the Logos. He is said to be God, but not the Supreme God. If we admit that He was in *some sense* Divine, or was God by office, or delegated power and prerogative, we do not reject this testimony concerning Him. Here we submit four short remarks. 1. That Christ was a creature in *some sense divine*, or that He was God *by office or prerogative;* and that HE WAS GOD; are not identical propositions. They appear at least to have infinitely different meanings, and wonderful must be the critical ingenuity, that can make them even *seem* convertible. 2. If the incontrovertible meaning of other passages of Scripture would be set aside by taking the words before us in their obvious sense, an attempt to interpret them differently might show respect for the sacred oracles; but there is a great mass of Scripture testimony demanding an adherence to the obvious sense in this place, and not a sentence nor a word to justify a departure from it. There are many scriptures which assert that Christ was a man, but there is not one which denies his Supreme Divinity. On the contrary, it might be shown, as it has often been, with the greatest strength of evidence, that this latter point is asserted in Scripture in the most unequivocal manner. 3. The first of these affirmations concerning the Logos, namely, that "He was in the beginning," prepares us to take the present one in its obvious import. If the Logos was in the beginning, that is, as we have proved the phrase to mean, existed before all created things, and, of course, was distinct from them and uncreated, there should be no hesitation in admitting his Deity in the absolute sense. After hearing that Christ is an uncreated or eternal Being, no surprise should be felt, at being informed that He is the Supreme God. The first of these propositions includes the second. If any thing be peculiar to the great Supreme, it is to have existed from eternity, or to be, without having been created or begun to be. 4. Since the words refer to Christ as existing in eternity, while as yet there was no world, and no time, to make them declare that he was God by office, is to forget that office implies creatures, over whom it is exercised. How was He God by office when there were no objects in existence to hold office over?

Zeal for the Divine Unity, is the ostensible motive for so explaining this and other scriptures as to disallow the Supreme Deity of our Saviour. The proposition that there was a Being with God, who was yet Himself Supreme God, implies, it is alleged, dualism in the Divine Nature, than which nothing is more contrary to both reason and Scripture. The implication, we reply, is not included. God may be one in essence, and more than one in some other respect. There may be a distinction in the mode of the Divine existence, and yet be perfect unity in the Divine essence. This is not in itself a contradiction, and if Scripture asserts it, the inspiration of the Bible should be disproved, before it is rejected. Further; there may be a distinction in the Godhead of *such a kind*, as to admit of more than one impersonation of it, consistently with its numerical unity. That is; the one God may be one in respect to Godhead, and yet more than one in some other respect; and the difference in this other respect may be such as to lay the basis for distinct *Personal* attributes and offices. This is not an inconsistency in itself: No man can show it to be an absurdity: No man can discard it as contrary to reason without making himself wiser than God, provided Scripture has affirmed it. If now Scripture has affirmed that a Person called the Logos, had union and happiness in eternity with God, and that this Person was Himself God, supreme and eternal, why, since God may subsist in several Persons and yet be one God, should we hesitate to adopt the belief that He does so subsist;—a doctrine, which, while it makes Scripture intelligible and consistent, in the present case, is demanded in explicit terms by a thousand other texts, and has ever been a fundamental article in the faith of the Christian church? It is not said, that the Logos *as God*, was with God; but that the Logos, as *the Logos*, was with God. When it can be shown that the expressions *the Logos as the Logos*, and *the Logos as God*, mean precisely the same thing, then may dualism in the Divine Essence be inferred from that interpretation of the phrase, *the Logos was God*, which gives it as a proof-text, of the Supreme Deity of Jesus Christ.

IV. We proceed to the fourth of these great testimonies. We are confirmed in the belief, that the Evangelist meant to assert the Divinity of Christ in the former affirmation, by what he now tells us of his agency. He makes Him the author of the universe—"All things were made by Him; and without Him was not any thing made that was made." If He who produced all things from nothing, be not the Supreme God, the idea of such a Being has not yet entered into the human mind. This is here said to be the work of Christ in the most emphatic and guarded terms. The universe in general, is first made His workmanship, and then each particular existence composing it, so as to preclude one exception.

It has been said, that the creation here meant, was the new spiritual creation; the state of things in the moral world, as arranged under the New Testament dispensation; and that the assertion of the Evangelist is, that Christ was in all respects the author of that state and order of things. But not only is this said without warrant from the context, but it would not have been said, had the preceding testimonies concerning Christ been taken in the only sense, in which, as we have seen, every rule of just interpretation requires them to be taken. It is only those who deny that Christ was, *at* the creation, and therefore *before* it, and Supreme God, who take the words before us as referring to the spiritual or moral world. To give them such a reference is taking such liberty with them, as no one would take, who had not some favorite doctrine or interpretation which otherwise must be surrendered. Besides, this assertion, so weak in itself, so unsupported, so repudiated by the context, is a virtual denial of what Scripture elsewhere affirms with the greatest stress. We shall cite a passage to this purport from Paul's epistle to the Colossians, and subjoin a comment. "For by Him (Christ) were all things created, that are in heaven and that are on earth, visible and invisible, whether they be thrones or dominions, or principalities, or powers, all things were created by Him, and for Him." "Not one example," remarks Whitby on this place, "can be shown where the creation of all things in heaven and earth, is ever used in a moral sense, or concerning any other than the natural creation. Moreover, in the first place, *all things in earth, and things visible*, must comprise things without life, the inanimate parts of nature, concerning which it is absurd to speak of a moral creation. Secondly, under *things in heaven, invisible, etc.*, must be comprehended the whole celestial hierarchy; but *good* angels cannot require a spiritual renovation, and Christ came not to convert *fallen* angels, but to destroy their empire." They truly have undertaken a difficult task, who are endeavoring to show that the Scriptures do not make Christ the author of the natural creation. It is the declaration of the Scriptures, that God created all things, but it is also their declaration, that Christ is the Creator; and since they teach that Christ was the Supreme God, they are not inconsistent with themselves. They likewise and frequently affirm, *that God created all things, by Christ;* but if while Christ possesses the Divine Nature, he is in *personality*, distinct from the Father, this expression conveys the sublime and most interesting truth, so clearly taught in other texts, that the Divine Person, in whom the creative power directly exerted itself to the production of the universe from nothing, was the same that assumed our nature and dwelt amongst men under the name of Jesus Christ. We forbear examining into the grounds of this economy of the creation, or searching for the reasons, why the creative power did not exert itself irrespectively of the Personal distinctions in the Godhead, or why the Person in which it did exert itself was the Logos or Christ. Tholuck asserts a necessity in this case. This only would we say on the subject, that if it were only through the mediation of the Logos, that the Deity could converse with created beings, or that such beings, as Lord Bacon says, could stand for a moment in God's eye, it seems meet and reasonable, if not morally necessary, that the power which was to give creatures existence, should exert itself in the Person of the Mediator.

V. The fifth of these declarations is, that in the Logos was Life. We are not to understand by these words, that the Logos was a living in contradistinction to a *lifeless* or *dead* being, in the primary meaning of these epithets. To say this after having affirmed that He was the Creator of all things, were not only unnecessary, but were to sink the lofty strain of the discourse almost beneath contempt. That he was not a *dead being*, by whom the vital universe was made, is an assertion which in the connections before us, no one can seriously think could proceed from the inspired Evangelist. But if *Life* here is not to be taken in contradistinction to mere *death*, what is the sense in which we should take it? It is not difficult to answer this question. There is a life, which is if we may so speak, the life of all life in rational creatures. It is not natural life merely, whether of body or of mind, but the higher life of holiness, or holy joy. Life in Scripture, often means moral excellence, holiness, benevolence; and often, also, happiness, the fruit or effect of holiness. These, from their relation to each other, are considered as one, holiness implying happiness as its result, and happiness implying holiness as its cause. We need not therefore in the present instance discriminate: life is holiness; life is happiness: no account need be taken of the difference. Spiritual life, including both true holiness and true happiness, things dwelling in one another as heat in the sun-beams, is the life which is here said to have been in the Logos. This life, which filled the rational creation, while in its first estate, and we may hope, fills it still with slight exception, had its fountain in Christ, as the revealing God. All rational creatures awoke into existence in possession of it, which along with existence itself, they derived from Christ. He infused into them the holy vitality which dwelt in himself and filled them with his fulness. That fathomless love which appeared so wondrously in redemption, had been before manifested as perfectly as the nature of things would admit, in the work of creation, when the morning stars sang together and all the sons of God shouted for joy.

VI. This history of our Saviour in his pre-existent state, informs us further that the Life, the spiritual life of whose nature and fountain we have just spoken, —was the Light of men. The sense of this statement cannot be misapprehended. We are in no danger of positive mistake, even if we do not fully and distinctly take the meaning, so as to be able to express it in a perfect definition. Man, when he first awoke from non-existence, found himself in a world furnished magnificently for his use, and gloriously illuminated by those larger and lesser lights, which still pour their splendors from the firmament. Those material beams, however, which gilded the face of nature, and transported the eye with the views of sublimity and beauty which it presented, are not *the light of men*. Nor is this the light of the *understanding*, consisting in ideas or the images of things in the mind and the results of combining and comparing them;—a light which may or may not be associated with moral depravity, and, if associated with it, is called darkness in Scripture, nay, the blackness of darkness. The true light of men is, as Tholuck has happily expressed it, *an ethico-religious knowledge, based on an inward communion with God, and comprehending the theoretical and practical at the same time;* a knowledge obtained not by mere intellection, but by the blended exercise of the understanding and the heart, when in agreement with the understanding and heart of God; the knowledge which fills the upright mind, by its inwardly apprehending and loving the Divine excellence. This being the end of all material and intellectual light is properly the light of men; the glory and joy of our rational nature. The source of this light, which shone in man at his creation, purely and perfectly, was in that life in the Logos, of which we have been speaking. It was the communication of that Divine life from the

Logos to man, that made him the subject of this light. Even as in the new-creation by grace, it is by the soul's partaking again of this same life in Christ, that it acquires the light of the knowledge of the Divine glory.* Human teaching may impart the light of external knowledge, the knowledge contained in definitions; but that sort of knowledge, in which the true light of men consists, is not obtained, until a spiritual union takes place between God and the soul; it is by virtue of that union, that the soul obtains those views of divine things with which it is transported on the day when it is born into the kingdom of God.

VII. This recital concerning Christ in his pre-existent state, closes with these words: "And the light shineth in darkness, and the darkness comprehended it not." No note need be taken of the variation of the tense, since, as it has been justly remarked, nothing is a more distinguishing peculiarity of the style of this Evangelist, than the confounding of the tenses. The scope of the context manifestly requires, that the past time be understood in both clauses of the sentence. The declaration relates to the Logos in his pre-existent state, and to man as apostate and depraved.

Darkness here means human nature amid the ruins of the fall. Darkness strictly, expresses a state, but the abstract is here taken for the concrete. Man in the darkness of his apostate condition is spoken of, as if he were darkness itself. This mode of speaking concerning depraved man is not peculiar to this writer. Paul declares that Christians before their conversion

* John viii. 12.

were darkness: "Ye were sometime darkness, but now are ye light in the Lord." The present testimony then, referring to man as alienated from the Divine life, and therefore involved in spiritual darkness, affirms the renewed love of the Logos to him, in these circumstance of guilt and misery. When by transgression he made himself darkness, He who was the light of his soul in innocence, did not forsake him, but continued to shine within him, to the end that he might recover himself by repentance. Through the period before the flood and through all subsequent time, man, a few individuals excepted, was darkness; but the Logos continued to shine in the world. He shed some rays, even as he now does,* among the most ignorant of mankind, enlightening in some degree every one who came into the world; but they were shed generally in vain; the darkness which they penetrated did not comprehend them. The Logos was in the world, but the world knew Him not; He came to his own, but His own received Him not. They preferred the creature to the Creator, the finite to the infinite, the visible to the invisible, through the madness of sin. The great mass of all nations made no improvement of the light which shone amongst them and within them, but as Paul teaches, suppressed or perverted it, through their unrighteousness. Even at this day the light is shining in darkness, and the darkness comprehendeth it not. Is the reader acquainted with no individual

* Some have thought that the *constant shining* of the Divine light, was intended to be expressed by the use of the present tense, in the first clause; but we rest not our remark on this criticism, for a reason before given.

in whom this Scripture is verified? Does not his own experience teach him, what the language before us means? It is true in respect to himself, that the light has been shining in darkness, showing him his immortality, his relations to God, his sin, his danger, his misery, the way of peace, and motives to effort, of infinite power. Is it not also true, that in this case, the darkness has not comprehended the light; that he has seen as if he had seen not, and perceived as if he had understood not; that his immortality he has practically disbelieved, his relations to God violated; his sin he has loved; his danger disregarded; his misery not lamented, the way of peace not pursued, motives vast as eternity resisted? Where is the man who can seriously reflect on his own moral history, and not know from an interpreter within his own breast, what is meant by the light shining in darkness, and the darkness not comprehending it?

Our reflections on these sublime testimonies concerning CHRIST PRE-EXISTENT, have deepened our impressions of the truth and importance of the three following statements.

First, That this world's opposition to the Christian religion shows it to be a world in rebellion against its own Maker. The Author of the Christian faith was the Author of the universe. The Founder of the Christian church was He who laid the foundations of the earth and meted out the heavens with a span. The institutions, laws, documents, doctrines of Christianity, rest on the authority of Him who upholds the pillars of creation. To oppose this religion is to lift the hand

of treason against the throne of the Almighty. The world have opposed and still do oppose it. "Theophilus of Antioch compared the little Christian church in the wide domains of heathenism, to verdant islands in a great raging ocean. Thus too within the pale of Christianity has the congregation of the regenerate always stood in relation to the children of the world."*
The testimony of this fact concerning the moral state of mankind, renders a denial of their deep depravity, their "desperate wickedness," the highest possible proof of it.

Secondly, That it is not Christianity, that assigns *simple* God-head or Deity as the cause of the creation. It is coming short of the teaching of Christianity on this subject, only to say, the universe is the workmanship of God. It is rejecting Christianity, in this great article, to exclude Christ's handiwork from the causal influence of the creation. Christianity tells us of a Logos as well as of a Deity, and makes the Deity in the Logos the author of the world's existence. They who assert that God apart from the Logos, or Deity out of Christ, was the maker of the universe, contradict the Scriptures in the most explicit manner. Intimations, that the creative power dwelt in a Divine essence which was pluri-personal, are contained in the narrative of the creation given by Moses,† and through-

* Tholuck.

† "After the closest attention that I can give," says Dr. Smith, Scrip. Test. Vol. I. p. 483, "the impression on my mind is favorable to the opinion, that this peculiarity of idiom,—(the use of plural nouns, especially *Elohim* in application to the Divine Being) *originated* in a design to *intimate* a plurality in the nature

out the Old Testament; but in the New Testament, the subject is set forth in the clearest light, and the express assertion made that the Creator was Deity in the Logos, or God in Christ.

The doctrine that simple Deity was the Creator of the universe, ought never to be published, and if published never received as a doctrine of Christianity; it may be naturalism, but it is not the Gospel. Nay, if it pretend to be Christianity, it is another and a rival Gospel, which no true friend of Christ can do otherwise than disavow and condemn.

Thirdly, That the greatest of all wonders is the Love of Christ for man. That our Maker should for our sakes make Himself a man—that He who dwelt in eternity with God,—glorious in all the perfections of the Deity Himself, and happy in the complacency of the other Divine Persons,—should, to recover us from sin and deserved death, take upon Him the form of a servant, and be made in the likeness of sinful flesh; and being found in fashion as a man, should humble Himself and become obedient unto death, even the death of the cross—

> "Oh, for this love let rocks and hills
> Their lasting silence break,
> And all harmonious human tongues
> The Saviour's praises speak."

of the one God; and that thus in connection with other circumstances calculated to suggest the same conception, it was intended to excite and prepare the minds of men for the more full declaration of this unsearchable mystery, which should in proper time be granted."—Any exposition of Gen. i. 26, or of the narrative of the creative process given in that chapter which does not admit this intimation, should, we think, be rejected as unsatisfactory.

V.

CHRIST PREACHING TO THE SPIRITS IN PRISON.

Ὅτι καὶ Χριστὸς ἅπαξ περὶ ἁμαρτιῶν ἔπαθε, δίκαιος ὑπὲρ ἀδίκων, ἵνα ἡμᾶς πρωσαγάγῃ τῷ θεῷ, θανατωθεὶς μὲν σαρκί, ζωοποιηθεὶς δὲ πνεύματι, ' ἐν ᾧ καὶ τοῖς ἐν φυλακῇ πνεύμασι πορευθεὶς ἐκήρυξεν, ֽἀπειθήσασί ποτε, ὅτε ἀπεξεδέχετο ἡ τοῦ θεοῦ μακροθυμία ἐν ἡμέραις Νῶε, κατασκευαζομένης κιβωτοῦ, εἰς ἣν ὀλίγαι τοῦτ' ἔστιν ὀκτὼ ψυχαὶ διεσώθησαν δι' ὕδατος. ὃ καὶ ἡμᾶς ἀντίτυπον νῦν σώζει βάπτισμα, οὐ σαρκὸς ἀπόθεσις ῥύπου, ἀλλὰ συνειδήσεως ἀγαθῆς ἐπερώτημα εἰς θεόν, δι' ἀναστάσεως 'Ιησοῦ Χριστοῦ.—1 Pet. iii. 18-21.

It is the design of Peter in the preceding context to fortify Christians against discouragement from the sufferings to which they were exposed for the sake of the Gospel. To this end he tells them that it is better, if the will of God be so, that they suffer for well-doing than for evil-doing; assuming that all suffering for adhering to the Gospel is suffering for well doing. He cites, in confirmation of this, the example of Christ, who suffered as a well-doer, the Just for the unjust, that he might bring us to God; the highest instance that ever was or will be, both of well-doing and of suffering on account of it. What the apostle would have them particularly remember was, that the sufferer in this instance found ultimately no disadvantage from the unparalleled injuries which He endured. Though He suffered to the greatest extremity, even to His being put to death in the flesh, the ignominious death of the cross, yet He was quickened by the Spirit, by which He went and preached to the spirits in prison, etc.

"This place is somewhat obscure in itself, but as it usually happens, made more so by the various fancies and contests of interpreters, seeming or pretending to clear it." The fact, however, that efforts to explain it have been unsuccessful, will not and should not preclude continued attempts. It is relied upon to support unsound and dangerous doctrines, and it should, if possible, be shown by just exposition, that it lends them no countenance. Its affirmation concerning Christ's preaching to the spirits in prison, is interpreted to mean that He went after His death to the abode of departed sinners, "the proper hell," and "that as He revealed here on earth the will of God unto the sons of men, and propounded Himself as the object of their faith, to the end that whosoever believed in Him should never die; so after His death he showed Himself unto the souls departed, that whosoever of them would yet accept of Him should pass from death to life." This and other dogmas contrary to the catholic faith, appeal to this scripture as their warrant, and so long as they do so, the friends of truth, certainly, should not cease looking for the key to its true interpretation. Whether there be any conclusive force in the following remarks, is with deference submitted to the decision of the reader.

We would first ascertain the meaning of the phrase rendered in our version, "quickened by the Spirit." So far as we know, what we take to be the sense of the original words, has never been given. If this can be established, we think a new ray of light will be thrown on the passage.

Our translation, it is admitted, is not the only one the original will bear. Nay, much as we desire to honor the received English version, we are constrained to say that it has in this instance given a reading which the original will not bear. The true reading is not, quickened *by* the Spirit, but quickened *in* the the Spirit. So it is given in Wickliffe, by Tyndale, by Cranmer, and in the versions of Geneva and Rheims, and so, but for certain theological antipathies, it would probably have been given by our translators. Both the prepositions, in the clause, "put to death *in* the flesh but quickened *by* the Spirit," have been supplied. The words flesh and Spirit stand in the original without any preposition whatever, and it is obvious from their antithesis, that if the word "spirit" denote *the active cause* by which Christ was restored to life, the word "flesh" must equally denote *the active cause* by which he was put to death; which, therefore, must have been the flesh of his own body, an interpretation too manifestly absurd to be admitted.*

The important phrase before us must have one of the five following significations: 1. That Christ after His death, was invigorated as to His human soul as distinguished from His body; that, though as to His

* Horseley.

body He was dead, He was more vital than before as to His soul. We cannot adopt this as the true sense, though the thing affirmed may have been true, for a reason which will hereafter be given. It may seem to be required, at the first view, by the law of antithesis, but besides that it is a feeble sense, it does not, as we shall see, fall in with the scope of the context.

2. That Christ, after death, was made more vital as to His Deity, as distinguished from His human nature. This sense must be rejected, as being inconsistent with the essential immutability of the Godhead.

3. That Christ suffered death, indeed, in His body, but was resuscitated or quickened again into bodily life, by the Holy Ghost. This, however true, is not what the words were intended to express: (1.) Because, as we have shown, the original cannot be justly rendered so as to give this sense; it must be translated quickened, not *by*, but *in* the Spirit. (2.) Because the resurrection of Christ was not more the act of the Holy Ghost, than that of the Father; nay, than Christ's own act. It is ascribed to the Father in Eph. i. 20. It is ascribed to Christ Himself in John ii. 19, and John x. 18. If it is anywhere ascribed to the Holy Ghost, it is not as His act exclusively or peculiarly; and no reason appears from either the text or context for introducing the Holy Ghost here as the agent in raising the body of Christ: nay, (3.) the raising of His body cannot have been referred to in this quickening, for the very reason that the context on that supposition cannot be explained. Indeed, all context, i.e. connection between the parts of the passage, is destroyed

by it. For what connection is there between Christ's being raised from the dead, and preaching to the antediluvians?

4. That Christ, after being put to death in His body, quickened Himself into bodily life by His own Divine power. This cannot be what is intended, because, to mention no other reason, the original cannot be so translactd as to admit the preposition *by*.

5. The only remaining sense of the phrase is, that Christ, after His death, was quickened in reference to His great work, the salvation of mankind;—quickened as to that efficacious agency, by which this work was to be carried forward;—an agency by which Christ made Himself to be felt among men in His power to save; an agency which diffused new and mighty life through the church, and, by means of His church, thus vitalized, throughout the world. This agency was specifically that of the Holy Spirit,—according to the representations of Scripture, the Spirit of Christ. So he is called in Romans viii. 10, and elsewhere, (1,) because, the Holy Spirit, in reference to the accomplishment of our redemption, is possessed by Christ above measure; John iii. 34, Acts xxxviii. Is. xlii. 1; and, (2,) because, for the same purpose, the Holy Spirit is given or sent by Christ; John i. 33, xv. 26, Luke xxxiv. 49. The distinguishing mark of our Lord, as the Messiah, was, *that he baptized with the Holy Spirit.* So He baptized His disciples on the day of Pentecost; and so, by their instrumentality, He baptized great multitudes throughout the world, or in the language of the prophet, "sprinkled many nations," Is. lii. 15.

Thus, though Christ suffered unto death in the flesh, in accomplishing the redemption of man, yet, relatively to that work, He was quickened in the Spirit, became efficaciously vital and life-giving, in the influences of the Holy Ghost, which were thenceforward so abundantly bestowed. In the Spirit, thus understood, he was "straitened" before His death, according to His own complaint, Luke xii. 50; after His death, He was "quickened;" life flowed from Him filling His church with vitality, and the world too became conscious of His life-giving energy, agreeably to His own forcible illustration, John xii. 32, "And if I be lifted up from the earth, I will draw all men upon me."

We propound this, then, as the true sense of the expression, as being, 1, the worthiest and greatest sense and on that account preferable, other things being equal; 2, accordant with a manifest and wonderful fact, which was then filling the world with excitement, namely, the outpouring of the Spirit in His divinely vivifying influence; and, 3, coincident with the scope, of the place, in connection with which it stands, as follows: No damage comes from well-doing: Christ suffered extremely on that account, and the result is known. To redeem man, He was put to death in the flesh; but His death was the means of life to His cause. Before He died, to use His own simile, He was like an unplanted grain which abideth alone; after His death, He was like a corn of wheat, which having yielded its life in the midst of a fruitful soil, is now producing a hundred-fold increase. To vary the form of speaking, He was *straitened* before He suffered; He was *quick-*

ened afterwards. Filled Himself with the Spirit above measure, He poured it out from on high, baptized His church with it, and diffused, through His church, a heavenly life among the nations.

Such is our understanding of this very important phrase "quickened in the Spirit." Irrespective of the light which the remaining part of the text receives from this interpretation, it commends itself, we think, as the only one the place will bear. It will appear, however, as having new claims to our adoption, when it is seen how it elucidates the following context. We proceed with our exposition.

The apostle having mentioned Christ's becoming thus quickened in consequence of His death, as to the life-giving power of the Spirit, goes on to speak of His having exerted Himself, in an office of the Spirit, among those who perished by Noah's flood. He expresses this in the following language: "By which he went and preached unto the spirits in prison, which sometime were disobedient, when once the long-suffering of God waited in the days of Noah." But why does he mention this ancient fact in this connection? What has Christ's ministry to the antediluvians, in the person of Noah, to do with the subject which the apostle has in hand, namely, His being put to death in the flesh, but quickened in the Spirit? This, at the first view, seems exceedingly abrupt, and some persons, probably, have been inclined by this appearance of dislocation and irrelevance to question, if the apostle be in fact speaking of what we have said, namely, the preaching by means of Noah to the disobedient men of this day. The dogma, as we have before mentioned, has been advanced, that Christ, after His death, went to the place where the antediluvians where now confined, for the purpose of preaching to them; and in accordance with it this text has been explained; and the explanation has, it may be said, this at least to recommend it, namely, that it makes the apostle less disjointed and incoherent in his discourse. For it is what one would be naturally enough led to inquire about, after being told that Christ, when lying dead in the grave, was, in spirit, more vital and energetic than before. Where was Christ's disembodied spirit, and how was it exerting its invigorated powers during the three days and nights which intervened between His crucifixion and His resurrection? An inquiry which it has been supposed the apostle, in the words following, proceeds to resolve. Is this so?

Was the soul of Christ in fact thus employed, while His body was in Joseph's tomb? If there is any testimony in Scripture in favor of this, it is in the present text. There is no parallel place, no hint, no trace of evidence, direct or indirect, besides. Presumption certainly is against it: for why should these antediluvians, above all mankind who have departed in disobedience, be distinguished by such a privilege as it is said they had? It is moreover fatal to this exposition, that it gives a feeble sense to the great expression, "quickened in the Spirit." The spirit, according to this interpretation, means Christ's human soul; but to say that Christ did not die as to His soul when His body was dead, but was rather more vigorous, were but to make a common place remark, and to say what is doubtless true of every one who dies, as well as of our Lord. We shall see yet further reason for not adopting this exposition.

But, after all, is the alleged objection against the commonly received meaning of Christ's "preaching, etc.," true? Is it impossible to trace a connection between this interpretation and Christ's being quickened in the Spirit? A connection there doubtless is, if the interpretation be the true one. Confessedly it is not apparent at the first glance, but may not a connection be discovered by close attention to the drift of the apostle's discourse, and by comparing scripture with scripture? We humbly hope we have made this discovery.

The connection in question is a connection or link of union in the apostle's thought, between Christ's being quickened in the Spirit after His death in the body, and His preaching through Noah to the Antediluvians, then disembodied spirits in prison. Can no reason be conceived of, why the apostle should mention these things as he has done, in close conjunction? We know the following fact, namely, that there was an important connection in the mind of this apostle between that flood, in foresight of which Noah, filled with the Holy Ghost, lifted up his warning voice in the ears of his disobedient contemporaries, and that eternal destruction which is now coming upon the world of the ungodly, and in prospect of which Christ, after His death, sent the Holy Spirit upon His disciples, and through them, thus qualified for the work, called men to repentance. These two floods, (if for convenience sake we may so call them,) though distant in time—the one long since past, the other yet to come—stood together in the apostle's illumined mind, closely related the one to the other. We see this in the following passage from the third chapter of his Second Epistle. "By the word of God, the heavens were of old, and the earth standing out of the water and in the water; whereby the world that then was, being overflowed with water, perished: but the heavens and the earth which are now, by the same word, are kept in store, reserved unto fire against the day of judgment and perdition of ungodly men." The flood of water, the first flood, pointed in the apostle's view to the second, the flood of fire, by which the world's final destruction is to be effected. He could not, therefore, well be thinking of the one without being reminded of the other. Now, this final destruction held a lofty place in the apostle's present meditation. It was to deliver men from this destruction, that Christ, as quickened in the Spirit, according to the interpretation of this phrase, which we have given, was now employed. This was the end of that movement now going forward through the ministrations of the apostle and his fellow-laborers in the work of Christ; and that the apostle had this in mind, appears from what he says in the 21st verse. Having remarked that the result of Noah's ministry was the salvation of few, that is, eight souls, by water, he adds, "the like figure, whereunto baptism doth now save us by the resurrection of Jesus Christ." Baptism, in its signification and design, was no other than the great work of recovering mercy, which Christ, as now quickened in the Spirit, was accomplishing among men. This baptism, not the outward ceremony so called, not the putting away of the filth of the flesh, but the answer of a good conscience towards God—this name for the great salvation now everywhere proclaimed, was the antitype of the water of the deluge—that water which, while it destroyed the world, saved, as the apostle affirms, Noah and his house. Baptism, we say, was the antitype (ἀντίτυπον—βάπτισμα*) of that water which floated and defended the ark while it submerged the earth. The antitype baptism, the great blessing which Christ, as now quickened in the Spirit, is giving to men—this baptism, saith the apostle, doth now save *us*—namely, those of the present generation, who, as did Noah and his house, have obeyed the warning voice of the Divine mercy. As the eight souls were saved in the ark, so we are saved by the antitype baptism, now appointed as the world's only hope. Another flood is approaching—a flood of devouring fire, which is to sweep ere long over the face of the earth, and dissolve the elements with fervent heat. In view of this overwhelming destruction, of which Noah's flood was a foreshadow, Christ, quickened in the Spirit, and exerting Himself in the anointed ministers of His grace, is rousing mankind from the slumber of sin, and warning them to make their escape, and proposing to them "baptism" as the means; and they who hear His voice and fall in with His proposal, are saved from this infi-

* See MacKnight's version.

nite ruin, even as they were saved from the flood who, according to the Divine premonition, took refuge in the ark.

We see, then, that this great destruction, the flood of fire, was in the Apostle's thought. Christ, being quickened in the Spirit, the religious stirs and movements of the times—the developments of the saving virtue of the antitype Baptism, implied this: but the flood of Noah stood in his thought, (as we have seen, and as it well might have done, from its prelusive and prefigurative relations,) associated with this other coming storm of wrath; it was to him a proof and a pledge, that this more dreadful storm was truly coming. How natural was it, therefore, that when he thought of the one, his second thought should have been of the other; that as he beheld the evidences of Christ's being quickened in the Spirit, in the great exertions which were then made to save men from the infinite destruction then impending,* he should remember that when the first destruction was at hand, the same benevolent Being (not indeed, as now, quickened in the Spirit, not in that fulness of power which He was then displaying, yet) by the Spirit in some measure of His influences, by the same Spirit, by which he was then striving so mightily with mankind, sought, through the instrumentality of His prophet, to bring the infatuated men of that age to repentance, and so deliver them likewise. And if it was natural for him to be

---

* Dr. Owen thinks the Apostle's primary reference was to the approaching destruction of the Jewish Church and State, but that he also embraced in his view the destruction of the world.

reminded of this, it is not surprising that he spoke of it.

There is one expression in our English translation of the passage, which some persons, probably, would lay stress upon, as being favorable to the interpretation which we reject: "By which, *he went*, and preached, etc.," (πορευθεὶς ἐκήρυξεν). But there are examples to show, both in the Scriptures and in classic authors, that no special emphasis should be given to this form of expression. Among Scriptural examples see Eph. ii. 17, "Having abolished—the enmity—and *came and preached* (καὶ ἐλθὼν εὐηγγελίσατο) peace to you who were afar off, and to them who were nigh."—"It is certain that our Lord, after his resurrection, did not go personally to the Gentiles to preach peace to them. He preached to them by his apostles only. But if Christ is said by Paul to go and do what he did by his apostles only, he may, with equal propriety, be said by Peter, to go and do what he did by his prophet Noah." He went and preached, is but a pleonasm for, he preached.

According to the exposition now given of the passage, the sense and connection of it may be expressed in the following paraphrase:

Christians should not be discouraged by their sufferings on account of well-doing. No ultimate evil will come to them from these sufferings. They may convince themselves of this by considering the example of Christ. In order to save mankind, to bring us to God, He underwent the greatest extremity of suffering, having been put to death in the flesh. Yet

His unparalleled sufferings were no detriment to Him in respect of His great undertaking. So far from this, they were the foundation of His success: all thenceforth was life in His body, the Church, and the world also felt His vitalizing power. By what abundant manifestations of the Spirit, and what glorious triumphs hath He since then been carrying on His mighty work of saving men from that infinite wrath which is so fast coming on the world? And this reminds me how this same mighty Deliverer exerted Himself by the Spirit through the ministrations of Noah, when the deluge was at hand. He then preached, by His faithful prophet, to the disobedient persons of that generation, whose disembodied spirits are now in the prison of hell, bearing the just punishment of their incorrigible impenitence. The great patience of God once waited on those unhappy persons for a long period, even one hundred and twenty years, during which time the ark was being built. The result, though small, was not an entire failure. Eight persons were saved in the ark by that water which bore it up and defended it, while it drowned all the world besides. The salvation of these few was the fruit of that same Divine grace which is now discovering itself in our deliverance from the greater wrath to come, and of which baptism, in its signification and purport, is the compendium; baptism, the antitype of the water which saved the family of Noah. I do not mean the external rite merely, but the thing thereby represented, the answer of a good conscience toward God, a conscience purified through the blood of Christ, and following its convictions in piously observing the sacramental ordinance of the Christian Church : baptism, another name for the influences and effects of Christ, as quickened in the Spirit—this antitype baptism, through the resurrection of Christ, which is the consummation of His work, and the grand proof of His redeeming virtue—baptism, I say, doth now save us from the coming vengeance of God, even as Noah and his household were saved from the flood which drowned the world, by the typical ark and water.

VI.

IMPOTENCE OF WILL:

WILL-NOT A REAL CAN-NOT.

God has given to creatures different kinds of power, or power to do different things. Reptiles can creep, fishes can swim, birds can fly, quadrupeds can walk: Men can think, reason, abstract and classify, discourse, discriminate between good and evil, can do good and evil, love and hate.

The power which creatures have by their nature, or what they are as creatures, is, strictly speaking, their natural power. The word *natural* is applied in scripture (1 Cor. ii. 14), to a man as unrenewed; but it is now used tropically; in its proper meaning it defines what pertains to the make or constitution of beings—their nature, as we commonly say. The power then which man has *as* man, that whereby he is recognized as man or human, is man's natural power: power to think, reason, discourse, distinguish between good and evil, etc., in short, to do whatever a human being as such can do by virtue of his having the human nature.

The epithet *moral* has been applied to power, and

so we have the phrase *moral power*; and it has been used as if it denoted the contrast of natural power; or, as if the power now called moral, was not natural, or did not belong to man as man. It should never be so used. There are but two senses in which it may be taken: Power may be called moral, from the sphere of its activity, from its being concerned with things of a moral nature, things morally good or evil, right or wrong. Power does not, on this account, cease to be natural. Power to think, reason, etc., in the moral sphere, is as proper to human nature, as aught else that belongs to it; nothing is more natural to man than this *moral* power. It is only by a metonomy, transferring the quality of the objective to the subjective, that power in this exercise of it, has come to be called moral. It is not called moral because it is itself so, any more now than when the objects with which it is concerned are not of a moral nature. Why should moral and natural power be made contraries, when moral power is still natural? Taken in the remaining sense, the phrase is figuratively applied to that which is not power properly so called; namely, to a disposition or internal state, whereby one is specially apt or propense to a certain use of natural power. One may name this power, if he will, but he does so by rhetorical license, unless he would confound a disposition to use a thing, with the thing itself. In no application of the term, then, is moral power a real antithesis to natural.

There is however a reason for calling *disposition*, in this case, power. Disposition, by continued exercise of the power it sets one to the use of, increases in favor of that use; and even by its first exercise may acquire a fixity unchangeable except by foreign power, as in the case of Adam in his first sin, who thereby subjected himself to a propensity to sin, not to be overcome except by renewing grace. It is not strange—it was indeed almost inevitable in a free use of language—that such a propensity or disposition should be called *power*, and there is no inconvenience from so calling it, provided metaphor or rhetoric do not afterwards pass itself as logic.

The essential difference between disposition and power appears in this, that disposition to use power in a certain way may be changed; whereas, natural power cannot be changed, without making the agent another being; in which case change is but destruction. A man as long as he is a man, will have man's natural power, power to do what is proper to a creature of man's order. In the great change called Regeneration, nothing in effect is done, but to bring about a new use of natural power by putting it under the command of a new disposition. The subject of this change, as to his humanity simply, is exactly what he was; he has acquired no new power, though from the new disposition which controls him, and the consequent new use of his power, he is sometimes called a new man.

As disposition to a certain use of power is not itself power properly so called, so neither is the hindrance to the use of power arising from an opposing disposition, properly called inability. Terms expressive of inability are often applied to it, but they are so applied only in free or tropical speech : As to effect, the hindrance is equivalent to the want of power, and is therefore taken for this, and called by its name, inability. We say the man cannot act, only meaning however that he is invincibly indisposed, or set against acting. The connection or obvious drift of language in such cases, generally makes the meaning unmistakable. When, e. g. the Scripture says that Joseph's brothers " hated him and *could not* speak peaceably to him," it implies, that their hatred apart, they could have spoken to him peaceably : they might have so spoken to him, had they not been otherwise disposed. They were therefore *able*, while unable ; which they would not have been, if the inability imputed to them had been a want of natural power : it was spoken of as inability by the license of rhetoric.

Nevertheless, this moral or figurative impotence, however denominated, is a reality : it hinders the use of power : if man were a brute or a stone, he would not be farther from the holy use of the power of a man than it is certain he will be, while left to himself in a state of subjection to a disposition to sin. Indeed, there is a sense in which this disposition may be said to be natural to man. He has it from his birth (Ps. li. 5.) He begins accountable existence with it, preventing grace apart. It is no part of the human nature as God made it ; is the effect of the apostacy ; but through the apostacy it is the sad inheritance of man, and may be figuratively termed a second nature. This the Christian ministry preach, as the fundamental fact on which Christianity is built. And it presents a question of great moment, as to appeals to natural power in preaching. Man is still man, a creature having the power proper to man; but, as to a holy use of it, it is as none, because of a bias or disposition to evil which underlies it; as it were, a second nature. Now the question just referred to is this: Shall we, on the ground simply of man's having natural power, urge the holy exercise of it, just as if this hindrance to such an exercise of it, did not make it certain, that he will not, of himself alone, exercise it thus? The certainty is known to us, and we endeavor to acquaint him with it; we state the evidence of it to him; we require him to believe it; we would have him feel as we ourselves do, that his existence is not more certain, than that he, if left to himself, will continue to exercise his natural power as he has been doing in servitude to sin. Shall we still urge him to the holy use of it, simply on the ground of his having it? Self-evident it indeed is, that he is under obligation so to use it; his having it involves this; he ought so to use it, and will stand condemned before God and his own conscience if he does not; nevertheless, if he is to believe what with so much earnestness we tell him, will he have any more motive or reason to exert himself as we require, than he would, if natural power did not belong to him? Though he is without excuse, though sin is *sin*, even when committed in a state of absolute despair, yet despair—the certainty of continuing in an existing state of sin—this certainty felt and in force on the mind, as in the supposed case it would be, is, by the unchangeable law of voluntary activity, no less effectual to hinder even the attempting a change of state, than natural impotence itself. Let the question be considered : Should preaching, since the fact is indubitably so, ever limit the ground of its urgency with unrenewed men, simply and absolutely, to their *having* natural power? Under the circumstances, what were more absurd than even an attempt to do what would be required of them? Nor can we conceive of their making an attempt in earnest. Palpably, therefore, they must not be shut up to this consideration, as a reason for their making one. There is, in truth, no persuasive force in it whatever, taken by itself. It is deprived of all such force by the pressure of despair. Some door of hope must be opened to effort, or effort will, nay, cannot but be forborne. The mind is so made that it cannot exert itself in such a case. Some other argument must be used, which will not leave the door of hope closed and barred. Along with natural power, mention must be made of some other power, whereby the holy use of natural power may be brought about. That is to say : the proffered Help and Presence of the Holy Spirit must be announced to the unconverted in the way of encouragement.

Let it not seem that there is no need of saying this ; there has been, if there be not still, a delinquency in preaching in regard to it. Has not preaching refrained, on theory,—from setting forth the hope of the co-operation of the Spirit, as a motive to exertion, previous to conversion ? By divers considerations, it has sought to set natural power into exercise, but the hope of the Spirit's co-operation, it did not, and, with theoretic consistency, could not, . insist upon. This co-operation was promised on the condition of actual repentance; but it was not held forth as an indispensable motive to repentance. The unconverted were pressed to repentance, just and only because they *had* natural power. Having it they were under obligation, and it was demanded of them to fulfill their obligation, to do their duty, because obligation and duty existed. With much persistency they were pressed to this; and the course was wont to be justified by its tendency to beget self-despair,— an almost phrenzy of desperation, wherein they might perhaps *break down*, as the phrase was, under a sheer necessity of an entire self-surrender to the Divine will, whatever it might be, concerning them. How strange the outrage which such a course obviously does to the principles of human action! What though grace be not necessary to accountableness? That is to say: What though the obligation of the unconverted have a sufficient ground in the fact of their having natural power, so that sin in all circumstances is inexcusable? If the object were simply to convict them, or break them down through despair, the course pursued might for that purpose have sufficed. But as the end which the preaching should have aimed at, was to *win* or convert them, nothing can be more glaring than the absurdity of this method. So far, this preaching was not the preaching of the Gospel: it was simply legal. The Gospel ignores and virtually condemns it.

But it may be that the day of preaching, of this form, is past, and that it need not have been adverted to, except, perhaps, as indicating progress. Be this as it may, there is doubtless room for progress still, both in the theory and practice of preaching to the unconverted; especially, it would seem, in regard to appeals to natural power, and the activity thence resulting, previous to conversion. Let this point for a moment engage our attention :—

It often happens that awakened persons, under preaching, in general sound, are perplexed with what to them has a formidable aspect, the alternative of either sinning or doing nothing in order to their conversion. They understand the assertion that "whatsoever is not of faith is sin," as teaching that all activity before conversion is sinful, and therefore forbidden; whence it seems to them, as they are not yet converted, the necessity exists, if their conversion is to have place, that it take place without previous agency of theirs, or by an agency which they ought not to use. Their case, therefore, is not, in their view, much different from what it would be, if they were thrown upon their own mere power, without the overture of aid from the Holy Spirit. As to activity or effort, in order to conversion, they are at an absolute stand. They must not commit new sin; yet, since they are still unconverted, what else are they to do, if they do anything? If they should hear, reflect, resolve, be active or exercised in any way, would they not herein be sinning, and so making their case worse? This is far from an uncommon difficulty, and there have been three methods of dealing with it in preaching. Some preachers have evaded or ignored, or possibly have not been aware of it. They have spoken to the awakened as if there were no cause or place for trouble to them from this source; as if their way could not but be plain before them; and, sometimes, they have pledged the promises of God to guarantee success, if they did but persevere in it. By others, to the demand from the awakened:—"How am I to repent? What way must I take? Must I needs sin or do nothing?" this reply has been usually given:—"I have nothing to say as to the How, or the Means of repenting, I only say, Repent, repent this instant, the next may be too late." Yet another answer has been made: "True, you will be sinning if you do anything before conversion, but you may be sinning more if you do nothing;" and assuming a choice of evils to be inevitable, that was recommended which it was supposed was the less sinful of the two. How plainly can neither of these courses be justified? The first is grossly discreditable to the pulpit; yet more so is the last, which expressly counsels what it admits to be sinning, as the way to conversion from sin, and that on the self-contradiction, that a choice between greater and less is admissible, where both are forbidden. The other, also, though under a show of logic, assumes what every one cannot but know to be untenable: as if there were indeed no place for preliminary attention, or thought, or feeling, where conversion has not already had place: As if, e. g. when the jailer asked with trembling and astonishment, "What shall I do to be saved?" Paul should have said to him: "You are sinning in putting the question, and in being excited as you are." Or as if Peter should have made a like reply to his hearers, when pricked to the heart, they asked, "What shall we do?" A psychological theory, or doctrinal creed which excludes such preliminary exercises as necessarily sinful, in this respect, most certainly, falsifies itself. The exercises in question are not spiritual, but neither are they to be rejected as necessarily carnal or sinful. The alternative of either doing nothing, or adding sin to sin previous to conversion, is without foundation or reality. There is no such alternative. It is not so that there must needs be sinning in all activity, antecedent, or in order to actual conversion. When God, seeking to bring sinners to repentance, challenges their attention, they do not sin in giving their attention. When, with reference to conversion, he urges them to consider their ways, he does not set them to doing what is in itself wrong. When convinced of sin, and alarmed at their danger, they seek to make their escape, and struggle against difficulties, and in their distress ask what they must do, and cry for help from above, their exercises, it is true, are not yet spiritual; but they are not to be on any account blamed or regretted; they are the regular response of simple nature to divine appeals to it; a response, of which the absence would be sinful. God surely does not intend to produce in us any impure excitement, but who knows not that He does address Himself to the nature He has given us; to every part of our higher nature; to reason, to conscience, to self-love, self-respect, etc.; and this before and with reference to conversion, as well as afterwards; and if the exercise of these elements of our nature in immediate correspondence to His addresses, that is to say, an exercise of them, which, like the addresses, is before and with reference to actual conversion; if this were necessarily sinful, is not God Himself, in this case, the responsible author of sin? We ought to respond to His appeals; we shall sin, with aggravation, if we do not; if we must also sin, when we do respond to them, has He not laid us under a necessity of sinning, and in truth incited us to it?

The importance of this point justifies further remark. The preliminary exercise of the simple properties of our nature, in brief, our natural power, is, in fact, the proper subjective means, whereby, through the grace of God, our nature recovers itself from the bondage of its corruption; and it is precisely this which suasory preaching, whether aware of the fact or not, aims and labors to produce in its hearers, in all its applications to them previous to conversion. In other words, through natural power exercising itself as it may without being as yet under grace, it seeks to bring men into a state of grace, the ultimate end of preaching. It does not stimulate this power to the doing of that, apart from grace, of which it publishes the certainty, that grace apart, it never will do; but to the doing of what it unquestionably may do, and of what it must do, as the condition of the removal by grace of the ground of certainty aforesaid, and a consequent just use of natural power.

It is of necessity that we take this course in preaching; we could otherwise do absolutely nothing in the way of earnest persuasion. How could we begin? Recognizing man as under a certainty, equivalent in effect to a necessity, of sinning, we should not be more incapable of earnestness in addressing stones or the dead, than in urging him to repentance. Earnestness depends on hope, instead of which, there is, in this case, by the terms of the statement, absolute despair of the desired result from the course pursued; it would be pressing men, in the mere exercise of natural power, to what it could not expect from them, as the result of this exercise: in this it is impossible it should be in earnest; it would be strictly absurd; and to hope for the divine co-operation with it, would be looking to God to sanctify absurdity by lending Himself to it.

Surely there is a possibility, a place of beginning, to earnest persuasion in the pulpit! Shall a theory be accepted which implies that there is none? Manifestly there is no such place or possibility, if man is required to look on himself as under the alternative of either sinning or doing nothing in order to conversion. Persuasion to doing nothing is inconceivable; and persuasion to sinning, is, itself, whether it means so or not, doing what it urges. There is, therefore, some form of allowable activity, which, though it is not spiritual, is not of the nature of sin. Man in a state of sin, and man in a state of grace, are, indeed, the two terms set before the preacher. Man has to start from the first, and not to stop short of the second. He remains in the first if he be not actually in the second. If he should die before completing the transition from the first to the second, he would die in his sins. In man himself, however, there is somewhat common to both states, namely the constitutional elements of humanity, or our natural power. He has this—otherwise he were not man—in both. He has it in the transition from the one to the other. In this transition he has and he exercises his natural power, which exercise of it is not already spiritual, else he were not still in the transition; yet neither, if the transition be transition indeed, is it sinful. But, on the contrary, being necessary to conversion, it is virtually included in the call to conversion, and the suppression or absence of it were a contempt of that call. This preliminary or intermediate activity, destitute though it be of spirituality, is the condition of conversion. Take it away, leave no place for it, and the Gospel and man can never be brought together, except by miracle or without the use of any appropriate means.

A word on the form of this transitional activity, or the particular exercises and efforts of which it consists. These, it is obvious, are different in different cases. In general they should be such, whatever these be, as are comprehended in a just response of nature to the appeals which are made to it with reference to conversion. These appeals are not always met or heeded at once. Nature, perhaps, is not sufficiently awake to recognize them. Perhaps they have to make their way against manifold impediments and disadvantages; previous instruction, argumentation, reproof, remonstrance, may be necessary; and after the contact with nature has been effected, she may be thrown into strife with herself, reason contending with passion, conscience with the heart, the will with interest; whence indirection, wavering, delay, obliquity in the course of the action. Such, more or less, is the general fact. Sometimes, on the contrary, the activity would almost seem to be normal or faultless. When it is so, the end is near. Nature cannot be true to herself without yielding herself up to the dominion of truth. Swift as time, now, is the progress to conversion. Let preachers understand this. Let them study psychology. Let them acquaint themselves completely with the many-stringed instrument they are required to play on. Let them learn to play on it skillfully, so that there shall be no discord, no movement too slow or rapid, no pitch too high or low, nothing but pure harmony, the sweet concert of all nature's powers and feelings. This should be their aim; with all possible earnestness, intelligence and tact, should they pursue it; never forgetting that to themselves and their hearers, the present opportunity may be the last.

But the whole truth has not yet been told. Where the response of nature terminates in actual conversion, the result is not from nature, but from the special grace of the Holy Spirit. It is not in nature to remove the ground of the certainty of continuing under sin. It is not in nature to do this, even under the best advantages of common grace. Though it is done through an exercise of natural power, under external appliances, it is not this that does it. Something happened to nature in the fall which made recovery impracticable by any merely natural operation. It retained its essential elements, otherwise it were no longer the human nature. It still was and is a living, active, responsible power; but as to a holy use of its faculties, it became blind, torpid, dead. Deep within fallen nature itself lies the ground of its certain continuance in a state of sin. A renovation, a "new birth" of nature is necessary, in order to render it properly susceptive of pure influences from without; in order, indeed, to its having any appreciative views of the objects towards which its highest activity is demanded.

The question has been asked: "Can man regenerate himself?" This is asking whether man can do a work proper to God. Or whether that which is begotten or born of God, may also be begotten or born of man. Man has no power of any kind, directly to regenerate himself. He is not required to do this, he is required to do only what he can do. He is required to be active in order to regeneration; generally—not always, otherwise no infants are regenerated,—but generally, he is active in the regenerative process; but the work of regeneration itself, is no more his work than his generation or creation. For this work man has no natural power. To reverse that law, whereby after sinning, a disposition to sin became as a second nature; to displace the ground in which this disposition is rooted; to put nature back to where it was before the fall, this belongs to no human power; God alone can do it, and it were absurd to set man about it. He may be set to doing what may be connected with it as a means; and what may result in it, under Divine direction and influence; and so, in a figurative way of speaking, he may be required to regenerate himself. The command of Scripture, "Make you a new heart," is equivalent to this: If men would obey this command, their activity would result in regeneration; having a new heart, supposes regeneration. But the making a new heart is to be done in some mode or by some means, and by a familiar use of language, that which is done in the use of means, is spoken of as if it were done by the instrumental agency itself, though in truth it is the product of the Divine power: as when we say, e.g. that a planter has made himself bread-corn, or a sick man made himself well; not meaning to deny that man might as soon make a world from nothing, as do either of these by a direct act of his own power or will.

What has been said on this subject may be briefly expressed in the following propositions:

1. Man's natural power is power to do what is proper to man, by virtue of his having the human nature, or being man.

2. Since the fall, the natural power of man is subject to the control of a disposition to sin, which makes it certain that left to himself he will remain in this subjection.

3. The Gospel bringing grace to man, makes ap-

peals to his natural power with reference to his conversion, or recovery from servitude to sin.

4. As it is certain and known that, left to himself, man will abide in servitude to sin, or an unconverted state, and so believing would, on the mere ground of his having natural power, be without hope from effort, and could not earnestly attempt it; he is therefore, not to be set to exert himself, simply on this ground; but, on the contrary, is to be animated to effort by the overture of help from the co-operation of the Holy Spirit.

5. All activity previous or preliminary to actual conversion, is not necessarily of the nature of sin: some such activity is generally necessary to conversion, and is therefore virtually required in the call to it. The activity which is necessary to conversion is not already spiritual, but neither is it sinful. It is not spiritual, because conversion has not place as yet; it is not sinful, because conversion is not attainable without it. The activity which, in fact, generally precedes conversion, is different in different cases: it is seldom, if ever, without much fault. When it is as it should be, it admits of no obliquity, delay, or wavering, but proceeds directly to its end.

6. When activity, in order to conversion, terminates in it, it does this, not of itself, but by a special agency of the Holy Spirit, whereby our corrupted nature is renewed and restored.

VII.

THEORY OF PREPARATION FOR PREACHING.

---

1. AMIDST the diversities of practice in preparing for the pulpit, are there no principles to be inviolably followed? Is there no theory of preparation? Undoubtedly there is; and, assured that the intelligent application of theory to practice, in this as in every other case, cannot but be useful, we shall attempt a brief analysis of our subject. If what we have to say shall incline none to change or modify the method to which they have been accustomed, our sketch may possibly be of some advantage to those who are yet to form a habit of preparation. We have to do with a difficult subject, and one which demands our earnest and patient thought.

2. We sometimes have to preach without having had opportunity to prepare a sermon for the occasion. The call is unexpected, but our duty to meet it is plain; and if indifference, or timidity, or a too scrupulous respect to reputation, do not hinder—if the love of Christ and of souls be the strongest impulse of our ministry—we shall in a few moments, be in the pulpit,

delivering a discourse, not from a manuscript or memory, but *extempore*, in the strictest sense of the word. We should not be backward to improve these emergent, out of season, occasions. They are probably among our best opportunities of doing good ; and the sudden demands now made upon us, may not be more extraordinary than the excellence of our preaching, if we meet them bravely and promptly. Perhaps, after our most elaborate preparations, we have never preached better than we shall preach now. We may outdo ourselves. We may have very unwonted if not supernatural ability for our work. Our speaking may be less our own than that of the Spirit of our Father speaking in us. We know not what unusual and wonderful experiences of Divine aid, what depths and heights of spiritual insight and feeling, what surprising enlargements of thought and expression, what special advantages for doing and getting infinite good we might resign, by declining to meet these abrupt calls to testify the Gospel of the grace of God.

3. It is the high and singular distinction of Preaching or spiritual eloquence—and this is our chief guide in the inquiry we are pursuing—THAT THE SUPREME AND DOMINATING PART IN IT, BELONGS TO THE HOLY GHOST. In the apostles, and other primitive ministers, nay, even in our Divine Master Himself, the sufficiency for preaching was from a special unction and co-operation of the Spirit of God.* In reproducing the inspired word by preaching, there is, as there was pre-eminently

---

* Luke iv. 18, 19. Compare verses i. 14, and Acts i. 2 ; 1 Pet. i. 12 ; 1 Cor. ii. 13 ; Acts i. 8, ii. 4. vii. 55, xi. 24.

in the first inditing of that word, a Divine-Human agency, in which as it was, in the higher case also, the Human is wholly subordinate and subservient to the Divine. The man in preaching is but an organ, though a living, free, self-active organ, of the Holy Spirit, who dwells and works within him to make him competent for what he does. The part of the Spirit in preaching is essentially different, and never to be undistinguished from that which he performs in original inspiration; but it is special and paramount; the preacher can do nothing as he ought, if he be left to himself. "We are not sufficient of ourselves," said a representative preacher, "to think anything as of ourselves." It is denying the substantive difference between preaching and natural eloquence to make the former the product, or a possible achievement, of merely human capabilities. There is, it is true, nothing in the structure of a sermon which is not referable to the human powers, as the directly producing cause; but a true sermon, is never produced by these powers of themselves; it comes from an exercise of them, originated, sustained and made adequate to its result, by a distinctive and special operation of the Holy Ghost. Preaching, the kind of discourse which God requires as the fit medium and vehicle of His spiritual power, is human, and yet not simply natural eloquence; the manner as well as the matter, the very diction of it is spiritual: "Which things we speak not in words which man's wisdom teacheth, but which the Holy Ghost teacheth, *combining spiritual things with spiritual words.** My speech

---

* See Calvin, Beza, and Hodge, in loc. The apostle dis-

and my preaching was not with enticing words of man's wisdom, but in demonstration of the Spirit and of power." A true preacher is a spiritual man; the natural man has no perception of the things of the Spirit, the material of preaching; he may have notions of these things and if he be an eloquent speaker, he may discourse on them eloquently; but he can make no spiritual discourse; this requires more than notions or forms of the understanding; it is from spiritual

tinguishes, (v. 12,) between *revelation* and *spiritual knowledge* of the things revealed; and here, speaking of the expression of these things in preaching, he says that this also was of the Spirit. He does not mean that his language in preaching was dictated to him directly, as if he had been no more than an amanuensis. His contrasting the teaching of words by the Spirit, with the teaching of words by man's wisdom shows this. Man's wisdom teaches the use of language not by dictating words to us, but by giving us through intellectual discipline and culture, the command of this wisdom's words: the principle of contrast suggests a parallel method, in the Spirit's teaching, as to words. The words taught by him in this way, are no less from him, than the words of which one has the use, through a liberal education, are from man's wisdom. If we are enabled to speak the words we use in preaching no otherwise than through subjective preceptions and apprehensions, imparted by the influence of the Spirit; if through the operation of the Spirit we accommodate the words to the subject, so that, " as the things we teach are spiritual, our mode of teaching them is in like manner spiritual," it is strictly proper to ascribe the language we use to the teaching of the Spirit. In a true sense he gives us this language though he does not pronounce it to our ear. But the apostle himself explains what he means by the Spirit's teaching him words, in the expression before us: " *Combining spiritual things with spiritual words.*" His preaching, both as to matter and expression, was different from ours in that it was in both these respects, *infallible;* but ours also should in all respects be spiritual, or of the special influence of the Holy Spirit.

discernment of the infinite things themselves. Preaching pre-supposes intellectual knowledge, but this knowledge, though one of the conditions of preaching, is not its direct producer; it comes from " a sense of the divine excellency of the things of the Spirit and a conviction of the truth and reality of them, thence arising."* There is the same essential difference between preaching and unspiritual eloquence, that there is between spiritual and natural life; only, as the exercises of spiritual life in preaching are, from the nature of the business, highly peculiar and unique, correspondently so is preaching itself, *the sum and the name of these exercises.*

4. We see, then, what a preacher is about when he is preparing a sermon. We have before us the sort of discourse he has set himself to construct. A different sort will not, cannot come from an operation in which the Spirit has the causal influence. Unspiritual discourse is neither from Him, nor will He take it as a fit instrument to work by, in effecting His proper purpose. He may, indeed, in some way make use of it. He knows how to use, He knows how to serve Himself of material uncongenial, and antagonistic to His purpose. Through His sovereign wisdom and grace He may turn an unspiritual sermon into an occasion of giving spiritual life. As by touching the dry bones of a prophet, the dead body of a man was once reanimated, it is not incredible that the Spirit may sometimes quicken dead souls into life, under preaching, so called, which has no soul-quickening virtue in itself.

* Edwards on the Reality of Spiritual Light.

But as He does not produce, so He never authenticates or approves, such discourse. However orthodox and eloquent it may be, it is not according to His mind, it is not homogeneal with the Divine nature; its tendency is not spiritual; and He seldom attends it, in any way, with His effectual agency. The sermons He is most pleased with are such as approximate most nearly to His own preaching in the oracles of God. In manner and spirit, as well as in matter, the Bible is the pattern, the exemplar to the pulpit. Secondhand preaching is without the infallible inspiration which dictated the Scripture; but the mind and life of the Holy Spirit permeate this preaching also. A true sermon is of the same temper and purpose with the Bible; the same in assimilation with the spirituality of God; the same in inconsistence with evil and vanity; the same in attractiveness to Christ and heaven; the same in antagonism to whatever imperils the soul and the immortality of man. No human preaching is perfect; but a true preacher strives after perfection, and the Bible is his standard.

5. The supremacy of the Spirit's agency requires the preacher, NOT THE LESS, BUT THE MORE, TO ATTEND TO HIS PART OF THE WORK. Though the sermon is, at last, the result of two combined agencies, the agencies have not the same direct purpose. That of the Spirit is not the sermon, but the preparation of the preacher. The Divine-Human in preaching is not, as to its ultimate product, altogether what it is in Scripture. In Scripture the Human is never the instrument of error; in preaching, as we just now said,

the liberty of man is not secured against abuse. The preacher, though a spiritual, is far from being a perfect man. His sermon, though made with the Spirit's co-operation, is his own immediate work, the direct fruit of his own labor. The Spirit does but help him to help himself; his freedom is not abridged; he has special assistance from the Spirit, but he may neglect and frustrate it. By inattention, by indolence, by haste, by self-wisdom, by ambition, by aspiring after eminence in his work, he may cross and thwart the working of the Spirit within him. Even prophetic inspiration left entire liberty to the will of the prophet. "The spirit of the prophets was subject to the prophets." More than once the anger of the Lord was kindled against Moses himself. No man should guard himself more watchfully against the neglect or perversion of advantages, than he in whom the Spirit is working with reference to his having ability in preparing to preach. Paul has left all preachers an example as to their method and measure, in the entire exercise of their ministry: "Whereunto I labor, striving according to his working, who worketh in me mightily."*

6. The nature of preaching as spiritual work—work not to be done without the co-operation of the Spirit—acquaints us with the part WHICH PRAYER HAS IN PREPARING FOR IT. Self-evidently, prayer, as a means, is required before every other, and is, virtually at least, continued and ascendant in every other. If a spiritual discourse is not a possible achievement

* Col. i. 29.

of natural power, to attempt one independently of the aid of the Holy Spirit were a plain absurdity; and since the Spirit is present to impart His aid, the attempt were impious, an insult to the Infinite Spirit, as well as absurd. But not without intentional and conscious effort on the preacher's part, directed to that end, is the power of the Spirit developed in congenial concurrence with his activity. The Divine does not concur with the Human in this free and holy operation, but at the urgent and continued exertion of the Human. Even in the ordinary work of sanctification, in which also the Divine and Human are combined,* this is the case; and may it be otherwise in this high and special work of holy power? May a man make a sermon, without consciously looking to the Spirit and seeking His assistance, when, without doing this, he cannot read the Scriptures, or do aught else as he should? It is an intuition of conscience that a preacher is required, by the business of his vocation, to be, above others, a man of prayer. It was but natural, the dictate of common reason, that the apostles should think of instituting a new office in the Church when they saw that otherwise they would be hindered in giving themselves to prayer and the ministry of the word. And was it with no reference to what was needful to ordinary preachers, that the pre-eminence of their Master and Lord, in connecting the practice of prayer with the exercise of His ministry, has been so particularly and pointedly recorded by the evangelists? What a lesson is it to common

* Phil. ii. 12, 13.

preachers, as to the place they should give to prayer in their plan of labor, that the greatest of all the inspired ministers of Christ, in nearly all his epistles, makes specific mention of his own habit in regard to prayer;[*] and asks so fervently the prayers of the Church;[†] and particularly, that they would pray that *God would assist him in the work of preaching.*[‡] Is it surprising that the great models of the pulpit had their fellowship with their Lord and His chief apostle in this spiritual habit? that Luther gave many of his best hours every day to earnest wrestling with God; showing thus his faith in his own motto (*bene orasse, bene studuisse*); and doubtless how he came to adopt it as his motto? that Whitfield's preparations were chiefly made on his knees at the mercy-seat? that the main business of Bruce in preparation was the elevation of his heart into a holy and reverential frame, and in pouring it out before God in wrestling prayer? Is it not manifest that this, in truth, must be the main business with every preacher who really regards preaching as an impossibility to man without aid from above? He will, of course, give to the work, study, invention, the closest application of his mind, the highest use of his talent, learning, culture; but in all, and more than all, he will be praying in spirit with all prayer and supplication, that the Holy Spirit may not cease to work mightily within him, illuminating, sanctifying, strengthening

---

[*] 1 Thess. iii. 10; Col. i 3; Philip i. 4; Rom. i. 19; Eph. i. 16; 2 Tim. i. 3; Phil. iv.

[†] Rom. xv. 30; 2 Cor. i. 2.   [‡] Eph. vi. 14; 1 Thess. v. 25.

directing the exercise of his faculties, until he has completed his preparation.

7. Advancing further with our inquiry, we come at once to the question : WHETHER WRITING IS TO BE INCLUDED IN THE WORK? Is composition essential to the best preparation? In the absolute sense, no ; but yes, yes, with emphasis, relatively to general proficiency. In some instances we may prepare better without than with writing ; we sometimes preach better when we have no manuscript, not even a brief ; but, on the whole, the highest success in preparing requires the use of the pen. "The pen is the best, the most excellent former and director of the tongue. However long a person may practice spontaneous elocution, he can never command admiration without practice in writing ; and the man who after using his pen shall come to the bar, will carry along with him this advantage, that though he shall speak without previous meditation, yet what he will deliver will have the air of correct composition ; and further, if at any time he shall use the assistance of notes, as soon as he lays them aside the remaining part of his speech will be of a piece with the preceding. As a boat under sail, though the rowers suspend their efforts, the vessel still moves in the same direction as when impelled by the impulse of the oars ; so in a continued discourse, when no longer supplied with notes, yet the remaining part proceeds in the same strain, by the resemblance and strength acquired from composition."* What is here so well said, has a

* Cicero.

special claim to the attention of the ministers of the Word. The discourse of the pulpit, more than all other public speaking, ought to be chaste in style and diction, as well as of masculine strength and force. The subject matter of it, the excellence and nobleness of its purpose, the criticism it has to meet, and, let it be added impressively, its great claim as of Divine-Human texture, demand for it, not only an absolute exemption from whatever is coarse, commonplace, provincial, but the highest classical simplicity and purity. What an indignity were it, to use the striking image of Foster, " to impose the guise of a cramped, formal, ecclesiastic on what is destined for a universal monarch." Moreover, the advance of society heightens the duty of the pulpit, to be in the advance, as an instrument of popular refinement and culture in all respects, and especially in the use of language, which besides being a mark of cultivation has no remote connection with moral improvement. The times require of the pulpit a higher order of discourse. One of the first thinkers and writers of the age, tells us : " It is necessary at the present day, in order to banish from the threshold of conscience, prejudices which to certain minds of a fastidious character, may be a lasting hindrance, that evangelical discourse should not be unpolished and rude ; it is necessary that, when compared with other products of the understanding, it should not appear chargeable with any kind of inferiority, and that no one should have it to say, with any appearance of reason, that it is only the ears of the vulgar of which it has the command. And let it not be imagined that the merit of an elaborate composition may be anywhere lost from its not being everywhere appreciated. In all minds true excellence and true beauty find a point in which they are felt. Their intimate congeniality with all the wants of the soul, enable them at length to penetrate it. The discernment of just expressions and silent forms gradually becomes an instinct with the multitude; and the preacher's care as to the logic of his composition, and the texture of his language, gives him a new authority over the people, whereby he becomes not only their spiritual guide, but, in many respects, their law-giver."*

8. It would then, doubtless, be perilous to the credit and honor of preaching, to forbear writing as a means of preparing for the pulpit. Few, even of educated preachers, men of literary talent, could preach no other than unwritten sermons, without incurring blemishes of elocution, which might seriously impair their general influence as public speakers. They would be in danger of becoming more or less inexact, repetitious, disorderly, if not even slovenly, not only in diction, but in thinking and reasoning also. This danger has been actualized in too many examples.

9. But it should be added, on the other hand, and with strong accent, that if writing for the pulpit be important, not less so ARE THE CAPACITY AND THE HABIT OF PREPARATION WITHOUT WRITING. Generally, indeed, this latter mode of preparation is a condition of the highest success in the other mode. Better that a preacher should write no sermons than compose as

* Vinet's Installation Discourse.

many as he will probably have to preach. Of three sermons a week, the least number usually required, he would hardly have time for more than the bare handwriting. Unless he has uncommon facility of composition, he cannot write well, more than one at the utmost. And the utility of the habit of composition depends on the care given to the work. Better that one should do all his preaching extemporaneously, than practise no other than negligent, hasty, extemporaneous writing. But what is a preacher's resource, if, having three sermons to preach, he write only one? Either, he must use other men's sermons, or repeat his own, or prepare to preach without writing. The first, however allowable, elsewhere, is inadmissible with us; the second, after a while will make his preaching insipid to his hearers, as well as next to intolerable to himself. Without great disadvantage and loss of influence, he cannot repeat to his stated hearers, more than once or twice, discourses which they will remember—" What eloquence is that of a man whose hearer knows beforehand all his expressions, and his moving appeals? A likely way indeed, to surprise, to astonish, to soften, to convince, to persuade men! A strange method of concealing art and letting nature speak! For my part, I say that all this offends me. What! shall a steward of the mysteries of God, be an idle declaimer, jealous of his reputation, and ambitious of vain pomp? Shall he not venture to speak of God to his people, without having arranged all his words, and learned like a school boy his lesson by heart?"*

* Fenelon.

The third is the only remaining means; *he must prepare to preach without writing.* Plagiarism and the too oft repetition of the same discourse apart, extemporaneous preaching would seem to be a necessity.

10. And this means, which there appears to be hardly any way of dispensing with, HAS ITS OWN VERY HIGH RECOMMENDATION. Along with the other, and in larger measure than that can well have, it enhances, on the whole, the utility of a protracted course of preaching. Indeed, valuable as well written discourses are in other respects, their chief advantage, ultimately, both to the preacher and his hearers, is from the influence they have on the preparation to preach extemporaneously. Certain it is, that the ideal of excellence in preaching, is unattainable when the delivery is from full notes.* Extemporizing in itself is the best way of speaking, the natural way, the only speaking indeed, in the strict sense of the term.† Each of the other ways, reading, reciting, reproducing from a manuscript, has somewhat in it, which nature would hardly suggest or allow in such an occupation as that of *addressing*, speaking to, an assembly.‡ Neither of them is often if ever used, in other kinds of eloquence. Does the singularity of the pulpit in using them so freely as it has done, admit of an apology? A great master in

---

* "To read in a manuscript book as our clergy now do, is not to preach at all. Preach out of a book if you must, but do not read in it or even from it. A read sermon of twenty minutes will seem longer to the hearers than a free discourse of an hour."—*Coleridge.*

† Whately's Rhetoric.

‡ "Nunquam aliud natura, aliud sapientia dicit."—*Juvenal.*

the ministry of the word has said: "The people must be taught in a manner that they may be inwardly convinced, and made to feel the truth of what the apostle says, that 'the word of God is a two-edged sword, piercing even to the dividing asunder of the soul and spirit, the joints and marrow, and is a discerner of the thoughts and intents of the heart." There is too little of living preaching in your kingdom (England); sermons there have been mostly read or recited. True and faithful servants of God ought not to wish to shine in the ornaments of rhetoric, or effect great things thereby; but THE SPIRIT OF GOD SHOULD BE ECHOED BY THEIR VOICE, and so give birth to virtue. *No possible danger must be permitted to abridge the liberty of the Spirit of God, or prevent his free course among those he has adorned with his graces for the edifying of the Church."*

11. This last remark of Calvin should be as a loud warning to preachers, when writing discourses for the pulpit. Both in preparing and preaching from manuscripts, there is special danger of ABRIDGING THE LIBERTY OF THE SPIRIT, in His part of the work. From neither, as we have before insisted, is His peculiar agency to be for a moment abstracted. Writing is the preacher's business; he puts himself in it, if he does it in earnest; and he is very apt, from the nature of the operation, to be in it *by himself,* and to do it in too exclusive self reliance; and when he has done it, to restrict himself to what he has written, ignoring the Spirit's province and right, in the actual work of

---

* Letter of John Calvin to Somerset.

preaching, even to the end. He is in peril of doing this in the other way of preaching also; but his liability to it is special, when he uses a completely written discourse. And he knows not what his preaching may lose if he does abridge the Spirit's liberty in it. By far the best part of preaching is often from the unanticipated assistances of the Holy Spirit. "The salient points of Whitfield's oratory, were not prepared passages; they were bursts of passion, like the jets of a geyser when the spring is in full play."* "The degree," says Thomas Scott, "in which after the most careful preparation for the pulpit, new thoughts, new arguments, animated addresses often flow into my mind, while speaking to the congregation on very common subjects, makes me feel as if I was quite another man, than when poring over them in my study." A preacher, whom we know, has related of himself, that when discoursing from Heb. xi. 5, he had such a sense given to him at the moment, of the patriarch's privilege there mentioned ("before his translation he had the testimony that he pleased God,") that he was enabled to enlarge on it, nearly half an hour, in an almost rapture, which made him nearly unconscious of what he was doing or where he was, yet as he gathered from a reporter, without inflation of style, or any kind of excess; making discourse, he believed, never equalled by himself, before or afterwards. There have been instances yet more remarkable—instances wherein the Holy Spirit, in the exercise of His sovereign right in the business of the pulpit, has displaced

* Southey.

altogether the preacher's precomposed sermon, by one spontaneously preached by him from the same, or another text. "The Rev. Dr. Dickson, handed me* on Saturday evening, his sermon for Sabbath morning, to read, and I went to church expecting to hear him preach it: He took the same text, but not one idea of what he had written and I read, did he utter. At dinner, he asked, if I had observed anything at church. Yes. What was it? Why, sir, you took your Saturday evening text, but you uttered not one idea on it you had written to preach. I thought you would notice it. I got such a new and precious view of my text, when in prayer, that I put my sermon in the Bible and spoke just as I saw and felt." It would be presumptuous hastily to refer sudden pulpit experiences to the direct agency of the Holy Spirit, but it may be no less so to determine arbitrarily that they are not from Him: they may be from Him; it is within His province to give them; and no *possible danger must be permitted to abridge His liberty.*

12. The very idea of extemporizing, supposes that THE WORDS OF THE DISCOURSE ARE UNPREMEDITATED. In this consists the difference between the two methods of preaching. The matter of an extemporaneous sermon should be as well prepared as that of one which is written; excepting what may be supplied by a sudden movement of the Spirit, the whole ought to be premeditated and predisposed. The only thing to be excepted is the language; and this precisely, the

* We forget the reporter's name, but the anecdote is authentic.

omission of the language, is what the term *extemporaneous*, when applied to preaching, signifies. The words are improvised; they come for the first time in the act of speaking. Preparation to preach extempore is sometimes partial; that is to say, certain parts of the discourse, definition, division, passages requiring special exactness, color and grace of expression, are written, or words to express them fittingly premeditated at least. But in so far as these parts are concerned, the discourse is not extemporaneous. To prepare to preach extempore, is to prepare without choosing or thinking of words, previous to the delivery of the discourse. The words spring into being at the exigence and command of the mind, in the business of speaking; they are born in the pulpit, of the nisus and exercises of thought: and it is best for the discourse that they should there and thus originate; any specific provision for them would require labor, much better given to the preparation of the matter. There is no cause whatever for anxiety concerning them. If the preacher be not disqualified in some other respect, he may confidently and safely rely on being supplied with the language he will need. He may not have at command the niceties, and delicate coloring of expression, which he might introduce into an elaborate composition; but these are not essential to good discourse, and perhaps they are not desirable. "Eloquence requires a more manly temper, and if its whole body be sound and vigorous, it is quite regardless of the nicety of paring the nails, and adjusting the hair."[*] Let the words then

[*] Quintilian.

be left to themselves: So the best extemporizers advise. "Digest well your subject, but be not careful to choose your words previous to your delivery; follow out the idea with such language as may offer at the moment."* "If any words of mine could be needed to reinforce the opinion of the most enchanting speaker I ever heard, I should employ them in pressing on your mind, the counsel not to prepare your words. Certain preachers by a powerful constraining discipline, have acquired the faculty of mentally rehearsing the entire discourse they were to deliver, with almost the precise language. This is manifestly no more extemporaneous preaching than if they had written down every word in a book. But if you would avail yourself of the plastic power of excitement in a great assembly, to create for the gushing thought, a word of fitting diction, you will not spend a moment on the words. Generally speaking, the best possible word is one which is born of the thought in the presence of the assembly."†

13. Should preparation to preach extempore include the preparation of a PROGRAMME OR BRIEF TO SERVE AS A MNEMONIC IN THE PULPIT? Not ordinarily, for the generality of the preachers. Preachers who are not afraid to trust their memories, find more freedom in delivery, when they have no paper before them; there is an interruption of the flow and continuity of utterance in casting the eyes often on a brief. Much more easy and agreeable is the manner of an orator, who, standing erect before his hearers in perfect independ-

* Summerfield. † Dr. J. W. Alexander.

ence of aid from notes, completes the delivery of his speech. This was the manner of the most consummate extemporaneous preacher to whom we have ever listened.* It is strongly recommended by other masters in the art. "If you press me to say which is absolutely the best practice, in regard to notes, properly so called, that is in distinction from a complete manuscript, I unhesitatingly say, *use none;* carry no scrap of writing into the pulpit. Let your scheme, with all its branches be written on your mental tablet. The practice will be invaluable. I know a preacher, about my own age, who has never employed a note of any kind."†

14. The reason for the absence of notes, is more decisive, generally, against introducing *prepared paragraphs and pages* into an extemporaneous sermon. The more elaborately they are written, the more ornate and exquisite their composition, the less their homogeneity with the ordinary strain of spontaneous, unstudied elocution. Indeed, it is extremely difficult to hinder the effect of direct contrast between the latter and these elaborate appendages. "It requires the practice of years, and I doubt if even that would generally suffice, to dovetail an extemporaneous paragraph gracefully into a written sermon;"‡ and to inweave a written paragraph into an extemporary sermon, would be a yet harder attempt. One may be assisted by the impulse of thought, or the swell of emotion, in deliver-

* The immediate predecessor of Mr. Barnes in Philadelphia.
† Dr. J. W Alexander.
‡ Dr. Alexander: There are striking exceptions however.

ing a written discourse, to produce an extemporaneous paragraph of a piece with the composition; there is no like assistance in the other undertaking; the passage in this is from the natural into the artistic, from freedom into restraint, from warmth into comparative frigidity. There is not, however, an absolute rule against the intermixture of written with unwritten language in the same discourse, either in less or larger measure. Some preachers, especially in treating certain subjects extemporaneously, have used liberally the labor of the pen in certain places, with much advantage; the general heterogeneousness of the two kinds of elocution is nevertheless undeniable.†

† Several modes of learning to speak well extempore, have been recommended by different writers. The best mode, according to Lord Brougham, is as follows: "The beginning of the art is to acquire the habit of *easy speaking*. In whatever way this can be had, which inclination or accident will generally direct, and may be safely allowed to do, *it must be had*. Differing as I do from all other doctors in rhetoric, in this I say learn to speak easily and fluently, as well and sensibly as you can, no doubt—but at any rate learn to speak. This is to eloquence or good public speaking, what being able to talk in a child, is to good grammatical speech. It is the requisite foundation, and on it you must build. To speak easily, ad libitum, to be able to say what you choose, what you have to say—this is the first requisite, to acquire which, everything for the present must be sacrificed. This is the first step; the next is the grand one, to convert this kind of easy speaking into chaste eloquence. And as to this, there is but one rule—to set daily and nightly before you THE GREEK MODELS." But is this really the only means? Should not the study of English and French and some other models— models of the pulpit especially—be also recommended? Diligent WORD-STUDY, apart from all models, should, we think, be also insisted on. One's vocabulary—the number and character of the words at his ready command—should be constantly husbanded

15. But to return to the preparation of THE MATTER in distinction from the expression of an extemporaneous sermon: This, we repeat, is the same, whether the discourse is to be written or not. The only difference is in the composition. There is the same analysis of the subject; the same invention and disposition of materials; the same array of arguments, divisions, and subdivisions; the same working up of the every thing into one compact organism, the parts set together in the order of climax, one growing out of another, interfused, intensified, concentrated, secured against dissipation and divergence of force from the one object of the work; in the one case as in the other; nothing omitted in the discourse, which is to be extemporized, except the composition. In neither case, must the preparation be permitted to overlook or abridge the liberty of the Spirit in the preaching of the discourse; His way must be left open to modify, or add to the matter, if He please to do so; but whatever the Spirit's course may be, the work of preparation on the preacher's part ought to be complete; as much so when he omits as when he performs most perfectly the labor of composition. "The sermon must be well and solidly prepared," irrespective of possible accessions to it from sudden impulses or communications of the Spirit.

16. With different preachers, and with the same preacher at different times, there is great difference as

and enriched. In connection with every means, and, as of more importance than all, the pen should be elaborately used. And, one thing more we earnestly recommend, namely, *the habit of using only chaste diction in common conversation.*

to SPEED AND RAPIDITY IN THE PREPARATION OF THE MATTER. Sometimes it is accomplished with a celerity almost equal to that of lightning. " There belongs to the human mind a peculiar power of discerning at once the entire nature of a subject;"* it is given to the preacher occasionally, to exercise this wonderful power; with the inception of the purpose to treat his subject, the plan, the *partes* and *sub-partes*, and the course of thought to the end, are already virtually in his possession; the preparation is completed in a moment. But generally its movement is a contrast to this electrical switness; often it is the extreme opposite. The first view of the subject is commonly confused, chaotic, without the slightest perception of method or order; a process of intellectual gestation ensues, including deep, intense, protracted thinking; struggles with obscurity and confusion; with objections, with half-truths and indecisive arguments, with erroneous or false prejudgments, with bad or imperfect disposition, with disproportion, disunity, disharmony, complication, in organizing the material. Such, for the most part, is the toil of preparation, the condition of thoroughness and success in the work.

17. There should be NO SPARING OR ABATEMENT OF PAINS IN THIS LABOR. It is generally the all in all, in extemporaneous preaching. The character of the utterance and the elocution, the merit of the performance, probably depends upon it. With few exceptions, the whole is done, virtually, when this is done. When the discourse is written, the antecedent plan and

* Isaac Taylor.

arrangement of the matter may be changed and perhaps improved in the work of composition; not so, in the delivery of an extemporaneous discourse. The delivery now is generally predetermined by the character of the antecedent labor. It is as the preparation: the preparation makes it. Now and then, it may be otherwise by some happy accident; but the exception confirms the rule, which virtually includes the delivery itself in the preparation: when this is finished, the preacher by examining it, may anticipate the estimation of his pulpit performance. If he would therefore be sure of preaching well, he should be sure of doing well the work of preparation. He ought to revise and scrutinize exactly what he has done, whether it was by the rapid or the slower movement. His swift preparations, especially, should be subjected to criticism. They may be less pleasing to him, if he return to them after a day or an hour or two: Perhaps their rapidity was from want of breadth or depth, or gravity of thought: But his most elaborate schemes may be susceptible of substantial improvement. After the severest labor, the best plan sometimes remains to be discovered. "There are plans which applying the lever as deeply as possible, raise the entire mass of the subject; there are others which escape the deepest divisions of the matter, and which raise, so to speak, only one layer of the subject."* But even if no change be made in the work, a revision of it will be useful: It will fecundate and inspire the mind more thoroughly.

* Vinet.

with the subject. It ought never to be foreborne if there is time to give it.

18. The preacher may avail himself OF AID IN PREPARING. Conference with an intelligent friend, comparison of his plans with those of others, examining the discourses of others on the subjects he undertakes to treat, may, directly or indirectly, assist him. But more important than all other means of aiding himself, is this one, namely a quickened consciousness, on the one hand, of dependence on the co-operation of the Spirit; and on the other, of relying entirely on no other human mind than his own. With these two consciousnesses, which generally are inseparable, and involve one another, his mind will have the normal prerequisite for its freest and best style of activity, and for its greatest effectiveness and success. He will not assist himself really by any means if he forget or intermit his sense of dependence on the Spirit; he certainly will not, by using the method or thoughts of others, any otherwise than as he makes them his own by his own mental rumination and digestion. Not more individual is one's own flesh and blood, or personality even, than the material which one naturally or honestly works up in the construction of a discourse. It must be his own as veritably as his mind is his own. He may use freely whatever he can obtain from others, when he has digested it and inwrought it into the life of his own mind; but otherwise he cannot use it without using what does not belong to him, and he will be a plagiarist if he takes to himself the credit of originating it, or gives it as from

himself.* The method which the mind truly uses, is one which it forms to itself by a kind of gestatory process; it may be suggested or given by another, but it is not mechanically accepted, it is received through the mind's free self-activity; it is from the application of thought to the ultimate intention, FROM CONSIDERATION OF THE END. Hence all the material of the operation; hence, also, the disposition of the material. This it is that determines the number and the arrangement of the parts, and the entire method of the work. The whole business of speaking is resolvable into reflection on what is to be done, and how to do it; and the first indicates the second; and both presuppose the free exercise of the speaker's individuality. Both will express that individuality. Following nature, no two persons do precisely the same thing in precisely the same way. The difference will appear in substantial as well as in minor particulars. Even miraculous inspiration did not hinder the apostles from doing each his own work after his own method and fashion.

19. We have nothing more to say of the work of preparing the matter of the discourse. But PREPARATION TO PREACH includes more than this—the preacher has to prepare HIMSELF as well as his sermon. And

---

* We see in the light of this fact how to estimate books of "skeletons" proffered as "helps," in the composition of sermons. Except as inciting the writer to self-exertion (and generally they do only the contrary), they are not helps indeed, unless they do, as is the case with some of them, the whole business themselves; when, if they are used, they occasion the preacher's falling into the snare of plagiarism.

this, after all, is the most important part of the preparation. "It is not so much by what he says, as by what HE IS, that the preacher may flatter himself that he does not beat the air. Before everything he is concerned *to hold the mystery of the faith in a pure conscience.* This pure conscience is the true force of preaching. A discourse is powerful from *the motive* of him who pronounces it, whatever may be the mode in which that motive expresses itself. A discourse is so much the better the more it resembles an act of contrition, of prayer, of martyrdom. The preacher should regard himself as a channel for what ought to be conveyed by him into the heart of his hearers."* Preaching presupposes a very peculiar habit or temper of spirit. Preaching is an action of the soul of the highest spiritual excellence, if it be rightly performed, but for the right performance of which, no ready-made discourse, however good, is the least security. The actual labor of the pulpit is as much a spiritual, Divine-Human work, as the most spiritual preparation for that labor. The co-operation of the Spirit has never been more necessary than now. Even if the words of the sermon have been prepared by His help, and are in themselves spiritual words, they cannot be reproduced aright by the voice without the continuance of the Divine aid. If the Spirit withdraw Himself from the preacher in the reading of the Scriptures, he cannot read them as he should. The words are spiritual, but not his reading of them. The repetition of words, whether from the Bible or the sermon,

* Vinet.

should be in the exercise of spiritual discernment "a sense of the excellency of the things of the Spirit, and a conviction of the truth and reality of them thence arising." There is no action more full of spirituality, more animated by spiritual perception in its highest degrees, than the just delivery of an evangelical sermon. The short-coming, therefore, in preparation to preach, however elaborate and complete, is radical, if the preacher has omitted to *prepare himself*. His preaching, after all, will not be preaching indeed. He may be very eloquent, the matter of his sermon very spiritual, but his preaching will not differ essentially from the speaking of a mere barrister; it will be as really of mere human ability or accomplishments. The barrister, perhaps, might deliver the sermon as well as he; the action in his delivery of it would have the same moral nature; the eloquence would be no other than natural eloquence; it would be void of holiness, void of spirituality, void of the peculiar influence of the Holy Spirit. The absence of the spiritual element in pulpit elocution makes preaching preaching no longer. Discourse bearing this name, with, perhaps, the highest linguistic and logical excellencies, and even having the most sacred verities of the Gospel for its matter, may be no less ambitious, no less studious of personal reputation and popular applause, no more in affinity with the inspiration and influences of the Holy Ghost, than the oratory of the forum or the platform.

20. The personal disqualification may include, if not a want of modesty or feeling, A WANT OF SELF-

COMMAND IN PRESENCE OF THE ASSEMBLY, a serious matter, if one is going to preach without notes. A slight discomposure of mind is enough to take away his ability to reproduce his discourse, even as a breath of wind on the surface of a lucid water will deprive it of its capacity of showing the images of the trees and other objects which are about it. And a man of sensibility, who has due respect to the assembly, and to his own position, is in danger of being thus agitated, especially in extempore speaking, however well prepared and practised in the art. Even Cicero has said of himself, and he told certain eminent orators to whom he was speaking, that he had observed the same thing to be true of them, that "he grew pale at the beginning of a speech and felt a tremor in every part of his frame." "When a young man," he added, "I was so intimidated, that (I speak it with the highest sense of gratitude) Quintus Maximus adjourned the court when he perceived me thus oppressed and disabled with concern." Heroical preachers, who have been many years in the ministry, are no strangers to this perturbation. "I am now an old man," said Luther, "and have been a long while occupied in preaching, but I never ascend the pulpit without a tremor."* Practice in preaching, to one whom familiarity has not made unfeeling, to one who has been growing in the grace which pulpit duty requires for its just performance, enhances, rather than diminishes, the liability to agitation at the out-

* Nunc senex et diu concionando versatus sim, sed nusquam suggestum conscendo sine tremore.

set of the delivery of a sermon. "The more a man excels in speaking, he is the more sensible of its difficulty; he is under the greatest concern for the event and to answer the expectation of the public."* Let one approach the pulpit with a matured sense of the pre-eminent sacredness of the position which he is about to occupy, the responsibilities attached to it, the issues of the work to be done in it, and of his own insufficiency for this work, and would it be possible for him to remain unmoved without more than human support? We are acquainted with a preacher who, after escaping, through Divine mercy, out of a state of spiritual decline, was so burdened with emotion in the pulpit the next Sabbath morning, that he could scarcely command himself, or bear his new experiences, though he had been fourteen years in the ministry.

In speaking of the high peculiarity proper to true feeling and action in the pulpit, the words of St. Cyran deserve, we think, the deepest consideration. "Preaching is a mystery not less awful and terrible than that of the eucharist. It appears to me that preaching is much more awful; for it is that by which souls are begotten and quickened unto God; whereas by the eucharist they are only nourished, or to speak more correctly, healed. For my part I had rather say a hundred masses than preach once. We are alone at the altar, but in the pulpit we preach to a public assembly, where we ought to fear offending God more than elsewhere, unless we have previously labored for a

* Cicero.

long time to mortify our spirit, and that pruriency which every one has to know many fine things, which is the greatest temptation that remains to us from the sin of Adam." Is it not probable that too much of the self-possession and familiarity commonly exhibited in preaching is to be referred rather to the presence of a manuscript, or to an unspiritual self-assurance, than to proficiency in pulpit piety and grace? It is not in either of these that the potentiality is seated, for spiritual activity in preaching; it lies, exclusively, in a habit of soul, produced and perpetuated with reference to it, by the anointing of the Spirit of God. We read of primitive preachers,* that they were men habitually full of the Holy Ghost and faith; and from the nature of the business which is done in true preaching, it could not but be, that a man so subjectively qualified, would have this fullness in special vigor and force, when engaged in this business. It is hence, and hence alone, that there is a security for that holy self-composure, that sublime elevation above all regard to self, and the fear of man, which is the condition of performing this business aright.

21. Having analyzed preparation for preaching, so far as it is common to both methods, we return to WRITING, WHICH MAKES THE DIFFERENCE BETWEEN THEM. The difference is not small; for writing, after the best preparation, is a long and painful labor. Writing is not a bare transcription on paper of what has been mentally prepared. The words of the discourse, as we have remarked, have not been prepared;

* John, Peter, Stephen, Paul, Barnabas, etc.

they are produced by the emergency of the mind in the operation of writing. Not more in extemporizing than in composing, are the verbal creations and constructions, the creations of the moment; there are not ready-made sentences or words for either. The labor of the linguistic work in writing, is commonly much more difficult than the labor of preparing for it; not only are the forms of language originated now, but new ideas and relations are originated also. "Writting is still thinking, still inventing, still arranging."* "To write well is at once to think well, to feel well, to render well: it must have, at the same time, mind, soul and taste; style requires the combination and excellencies of all the intellectual powers. The intellectual excellencies which it contains, all the relations of which it consists, are so many truths not less useful, and perhaps of more value to the human mind, than those which form the foundation of the subject."†

22. The usefulness of writing depends ON ITS BEING DONE WITH CARE. Writing is useful as a gymnastic of the mind, that is to say, when the mind acts as an athlete, when its utmost abilities are put forth: writing again is useful as contributing to the command of language; as a means of chastening, purifying, and invigorating style, of improvement in disposition and method, of thoroughness in the treatment and exhibition of subjects, and, chiefly, as we have said already, of proficiency in extemporizing. But the writing which subserves these ends, is no other than elaborate composition; the fruit of a struggle after ideal excel-

* Vinet. † Buffon.

lence. We cannot retract what we have said: Better be restricted to preparation for preaching extempore, than fall into a habit of preparing by unstudious, superficial, extemporaneous writing.

23. But it is to be kept vividly and constantly before the mind, in writing for the pulpit, that there is A FUNDAMENTAL SPECIALITY IN THIS KIND OF COMPOSITION. It approaches as nearly as possible to the style of extemporaneous speaking. In its ideal, preaching is, as we have before said, extemporaneous as to its language; the extemporaneous sermon, therefore, abstracting its faults, is the model as to the style and diction of one which is to be written; it gives command in the verbal construction of the sermon. The pen, in composition, should as much as possible do the very office of the tongue in its unpremeditated utterances. It should intend the words it writes, not for the eye, but the ear. The preacher should imagine the assembly he is to address to be present with him where he is writing, and make his silent sentences and words as a tongue or a living voice wherewith he speaks to it. He must write in a style, analogous, not to a miniature, but to the bold representations of scene-painting. He has lost the idea of preaching if he think it realizable in a composition suited peculiarly to the press. The composition of a sermon should, if possible, be made perfect in its kind; but its kind is its own, and unchangeable. The style of the sermon, like its matter and its purpose, is individual and unique.

24. But, moreover, and infinitely more important: Writing for the pulpit should, no less than the ante-

cedent preparation for writing, BE KEPT UNDER THE COMMAND AND CONTROL OF THE HOLY SPIRIT. Not less needful now is the Spirit's co-operation : if possible it is more needful. There is special danger of being unspiritual in this part of the labor: the danger of the undue pursuit of ornament ; of ambitious oratory ; of going into a search for the enticing words of man's wisdom ; of depending too much on the sermons or plans of others ; of being too speculative and abstruse, or, on the other hand, vulgar and commonplace ; of being only half or almost true : in a word, of ignoring the Spirit's part in preaching, and, consequently, of abating the necessity and exercise of prayer. In writing, much more than in the preliminary labor, and than in extemporizing, the mind busies itself about the externalities, the outward investments of the matter ; in the other operation, it is engrossed with the matter alone ; or if it apply itself at all to the clothing of its thoughts, it does so for the most part, in an embryotic manner ; there is no distinct construction, or discernment of forms of language. The mind certainly can and often does think in these forms, but if it never thinks without them, they are often undistinguishable even in its own consciousness. It is at least certain, that whereas in writing, the expression is very apt to be the principal thing, it is comparatively as nothing in the direct activity of the extempore speaker. And this shows the specially high place which prayer should have in writing sermons : it is, if possible, more important now than in preparing the matter. The expression of a written, no less than a spoken sermon, ought to be spiritual, but where it is the chief object of attention, there is special danger that it will not be; it will be from special spirituality in the writer of the sermon if the structure and tissue of it be not unspiritual; in wisdom of words, rather than in demonstration of the Spirit and of power.

25. The work of composition generally goes on better when, without anxious attention to diction, THE PEN OF THE WRITER MOVES SWIFTLY, UNDER THE IMPULSE OF STRONG AND VIVID CONCEPTIONS OF THE SUBJECT. Direct study of expression at the time of writing is seldom the best method of success in the style of a composition. Quintilian tells us, that the choicest expressions are, for the most part, adherent to things, and are seen in their own light; while we search after them as if they were hiding and stealing themselves away from us. Still we know that one may have vigorous conceptions without ability to express them well; there are very good thinkers who are not good writers. Again, it is a matter of experience, that after the best preparation of the matter one can make, he has sometimes to depend on the labor of expression at the moment of performing it, to give him the precise conceptions he needs in order to write well. It is so sometimes in speaking extempore; it is oftener so in writing. The movement of the tongue in the former, and much more of the pen in the latter, is deliberate and interrupted; the expression being studied as a means of more distinctness of thought. But, generally, good writers and speakers give their direct attention to thought first and chiefly: leaving expression to

come at the nisus, and, as it were, the call of thought. The opposite order, the study of expression chiefly, produces a style not without ideas altogether, but " with ideas of tinsel, ideas without roots and without power; or, if some thought is mixed with it, it is external to the subject, sustained by nothing, and unsustained."* A vigorous style is from strong and vigorous thinking, directed to the matter, not to the diction. " A true style is not the mask but the physiognomy of thought; it comes from thought, as complexion comes from the blood, as the flower springs from the sap." This tells tells us why it is that very masculine writing is sometimes slow, very slow, perhaps, in its progress. It nevertheless remains a fact, that one ordinarily writes best, especially if he is occupied on a sermon, which should always have a popular, speaking style, when inspired and stimulated by clear views of his subject; his pen is nimble and brisk, and yet perhaps much too slow for the movement of his mind.†

But though with the generality of preachers, the rule in writing a sermon should be to despatch it, *currente calamo*, yet they should not assume that because they have followed the best method, and probably produced a better composition than they could have otherwise done, they should not subject it to A CRITICAL REVISION OF THE LANGUAGE, now that it is substantially finished according to the true rule. Verbal criticism has been biding its time; after a little rest

* Vinet.
† Dr. Alexander's chief trouble in writing was the time required in the chirography.

from the labor of composition, this second labor may be instituted, not only without peril, but probably with much advantage, to the fruit of the first. The first words, and the first verbal constructions are not always the best, even when the writer's mind is pregnant and aglow with clear and vigorous thought: there may be epithets too many or too few, or not well selected; sentences involved; redundant phrases; statements exaggerated or imprecise, or weak through too much strength; or without verity to thought. If the criticism keeps itself under the law which every thing in a sermon should obey—the law which makes subservience to the end the critic of every sentence and word—it can hardly be too severe. If it do not make too large a demand on time, it should not rest until it has done its work as exactly and completely as possible. Not only the improvement of the discourse, but the preacher's general improvement in the use of the language, is the fruit of fidelity in this second labor of composition. It has been of high value with the best thinkers and writers. John Foster, speaking of one of his own discourses, says: "I dare say I could point out scores of sentences, *each* one of which has cost me several hours of the utmost exertion of my mind to put it in the state in which it now stands, after putting it in several other forms, to each one of which I saw some precise objection, which I could at the time have very distinctly assigned." Robert Hall (witness what his biographer says of his toil in preparing his sermons for the press*) was scarcely be-

* " Writing, improving, rejecting the improvement; seeking

hind his eminent contemporary in this exquisite care for perfect expression.

26. But to return to the first operation: If the theory of writing well forbids the study of words, as the first thing, much more does it forbid the labor of PATCH-WORK in the composition.* Those who write detached passages at different times never combine them, we are told,† without forced transitions; and if they have trouble with passages of their own writing they will, doubtless, have more in working up excerpts from scrap-books, or memory, gathered in reading. The construction of discourse is accretive, not mechanical; never by mere juxtaposition or accession. It is the development of a living germ, an upspring and a growth from a living seed of truth. It takes nothing into itself from without which it cannot assimilate; it avoids heterogeneous, immiscible matter, as it were by instinct, as the animal in its pasture avoids the herbage which does not suit its hunger. The advance of a discourse to completion, and especially a sermon, a Divine-Human discourse, is from within outward; what comes into it from without does so by elective affinity, and coalesces with its life as it enters, so that this, with the rest, works as an inward living force. Come whence or how it may,

---

another; rejecting it; recasting whole sentences and pages; often recurring precisely to the original phraseology; and still oftener repenting, when it was too late, that he had not done so."—*Dr. Gregory's Memoirs.*

* " Purpureus, late qui splendeat, unus et alter
     Assuitur paunus."

† Buffon.

it will receive it into itself, if it will at once mix and become consubstantial with its own life; but it can accept of nothing which is not closely akin and germane to itself, however beautiful or sublime.

27. It is inexpedient to attempt a sermon which is to be written for an urgent occasion, ON A THEME NOT ALREADY FAMILIAR TO THE PREACHER. His knowledge of it should be adequate before he begins the work. The delay required by having to gain new knowledge, is incompatible with the intense and rapid thinking which is the ordinary condition of life and energy in the composition, and in the present case, probably, a stern necessity. He has no time to give to "reading up," or the acquisition of knowledge. He should have a sufficiency of knowledge when he begins. If more come to him as he proceeds, it should come spontaneously, or from the principle of association or suggestion, not by any direct effort to obtain it. By turning aside to look into commentaries or books of sermons, or even by stopping to ask information of a friend who is near, he is in danger of losing interest in his work and breaking the vital force and connection of his thought. He cannot do two things at once; he has time for but one; and if he had more time, the law of the main labor he is engaged in would forbid the appropriation of it to aught else until that labor is finished.

28. And one thing more as to the selection of a favorable topic. The highest success in writing requires a QUICKENED INTEREST IN THE SUBJECT AS WELL AS SUFFICIENT KNOWLEDGE OF IT. Eloquence is not

from knowledge or thinking merely, but from sympathy, from lively emotion, from light within, which burns as it shines. Eloquence is the fruit of an engagement of the powers and forces of the mind, in a business operation, an affair of action, directed to an immediate object. Interest is its law, its spring, its life; other things being equal, the livelier the interest, the higher the strain of eloquence. The preacher should, as much as possible, be impassionated by the subject, should put himself wholly into it, so as to be able to give himself to his hearers in and with his discourse. This is the condition of the highest success in writing for the pulpit; and it shows, what Pastoral Theology teaches as one of its great axioms, the CLOSE ASSOCIATION OF EXCELLENCE IN THE PREACHING OF A PASTOR WITH FIDELITY IN THE CARE OF SOULS. The best parish preacher is not one so engrossed in preparing his sermons that he can earnestly do little else; but one, on the contrary, so occupied in the work of pastoral oversight that his abounding in that work, his intimate acquaintance with the state of his flock thence resulting, gives him the word of command in the selection of his topics for preaching, and stimulates and guides him in writing his discourses. This is, in truth, the pastor's chief labor; that which, with a conscientious pastor, holds the highest place. "I confess I would rather hear the care of souls objected against preaching, than preaching against the care of souls. I would rather one should say to me, my sick, my poor, my scattered sheep require me, and forbid me to give my preaching all the attention which is desirable."* But there is no clashing between the two works: they aid, use, one another. Preaching serves itself greatly of parochial assiduity. Next to prayer and the co-operation of the Holy Spirit, the most effective assistance in writing for the pulpit is afforded by acquaintance and sympathy with the state of families and individuals in the parish. In this, as in everything, duty is one in effect with expediency and success. The secret of life, alacrity, excellence, happiness, in preaching is self-devotedness, earnestness, and particularity of concern in the pastoral care. The difference between a ministry of the word which springs from this concern and fulfills its impulses, and one which may be designated a ministry at large, is often as the difference between liberty and servitude, delight and drudgery, strength and weakness, success and failure.†

29. We here finish our outline of this important subject, feeling that, even as an outline, it is very, very incomplete, and hoping that if what we have said shall have no other good result, it may induce some one better furnished for the work to supply its defects, correct its faults, and extend it into a book. We feel that our subject deserves to be treated at large; it has not been so treated, so far as we know. Vinet

---

* Vinet. Past. Theol.

† "I acknowledge that there are two things whereby I regulate my work in the whole course of my ministry: To impart those truths of *whose power I have had, in some measure, a real experience;* and to press those duties *which present occasions, temptations and other circumstances, do render necessary to be attended to in a peculiar manner.*"—Dr. Owen.

seems to have included it in the plan of his great work on Homiletics;* but it has no place in that work; and we should rejoice greatly to know that a vigorous thinker, with a strong and full apprehension of the New Testament idea of preaching, with adequate learning and culture, and in special communion with the Holy Spirit, has given himself to the labor of preparing for the press a complete treatise on it. In the plan of our Lord for recovering the world to Himself, the pulpit remains ascendant over all other means; and let means be multiplied or varied as they may, it will so remain; and if it abdicate its place, or become essentially different from what it was at first, other means, however diligently used, will become as waters which have no fountain, or as bitter waters flowing from a fountain which has been poisoned. Next to the outpouring of the Spirit upon her general membership, the Church has no interest so momentous as the ministry of the Word. Amid the radical errors and misbeliefs of the times, are there no indications that the appearance of such a book as we have expressed a desire to see, would be seasonable?

*See page 261.

VIII.

DELIVERY IN PREACHING.

---

1. An intelligent observer of the common preaching of the times, who compares it with the New Testament idea of preaching, or attempts to resolve it into its proper principles as claiming to be a species of public eloquence, cannot but see that in several radical respects, it needs to be reformed. He must remark in it as quite ordinary and prominent features, violations of oratorical unity; want of the freeness, directness and pungency of appeal which individuate the oratorical style; want of the impassionate, the unction, and the agonistic force by which the oratory of the pulpit, more than any other, should be characterized. But with a just estimation of its share of importance in preaching, must he not, above all, note and lament an imperative demand for reformation in the particular which forms the subject of this article? Long ago, the pulpit was reproached very sharply for a very bad manner of delivery. Said a celebrated ecclesiastic to a celebrated actor of the former century: "How is it that you who deal in nothing but fiction

can so affect your audience as to throw them into tears, while we who deliver the most awful truths can scarcely produce any effect whatever?" "Here," replied the actor, "lies the secret: *you deliver your truths as if they were fictions; but we deliver our fictions as if they were truths.*" There has been, it would seem, no material change for the better. It has been recently remarked,* that action in speaking generally is so little approved or designedly employed, that it is hardly any part of the orator's art. In reference to preaching, the fact has been spoken of thus: "Why are we natural everywhere but in the pulpit? Why this *holoplexia* on sacred occasions alone? Why call in the aid of paralysis to piety? Is it a rule of oratory to handle the most sublime truths in the driest manner? Is sin to be taken from men, as Eve was from Adam, by casting them into a deep slumber?" †

2. THIS IS NOT A MATTER OF SMALL MOMENT. If preaching be indeed a kind of eloquence, and if its efficacy depend at all on its being true to its principles as such, nothing relating to the practice of it is weightier. Delivery comprehends all the modes of expression in public speaking. "It is," says Cicero, very admirably, "*the eloquence of the body;* and implies the proper management of the voice and gesture." According to the masters of the art and practice of speaking, it is the chief thing in eloquence. "What we have composed," says Quintilian, "is not of so much consequence as how it is delivered; because every one is affected in proportion as he is made to hear.

* By Archbishop Whately. † Sidney Smith.

There is no proof so strong but it will lose its force unless it is aided by an emphatic tone in the speaker; and all passions must become languid unless spirited-up by the voice and countenance and attitude of the body." In like manner, Cicero gives more importance to delivery, than, apart from it, to what is delivered. "Without a good delivery, the best speaker can have no name, and with it, a middling one can obtain the highest." Demosthenes goes further: "Being asked what was the greatest excellency in oratory, he not only gave the preference to delivery, but assigned to it the second and the third place; whereby it appeared that he judged it not so much the principal, as the only excellency." His own practice accorded, it would seem, with his judgment. "After Æschines had lost a cause, he retired in disgrace from Athens to Rhodes, where, at the request of the Rhodians, he read to them that fine oration which Demosthenes had pronounced against Ctesiphon, which he did with a charming voice. When everybody was expressing their applause: 'How would you have applauded,' says he, 'if you had heard the author himself deliver it?' Whereby it appears what a vast influence action had, since the change of the actor could make the same speech appear in quite a different light."* Let us not wonder at this estimation of this part of oratory. Who that has been much employed in speaking has not often found a good discourse spoiled, and a poor one made quite a success, by the manner of pronouncing it? The preaching of White-

* Cicero de Oratore.

field, apart from his delivery, was in no respect extraordinary; including his delivery, it has never been equalled. "To ignorant and semi-barbarous men," said John Foster, "even common truths, in Whitefield's preaching, seemed to strike on them in fire and light."

3. IN THE TONES OF THE VOICE ALONE THERE ARE ELEMENTS OF ELOQUENCE OF INCONCEIVABLE FORCE. The human voice and the human mind, both inscrutable marvels of divine handiwork, were made for one another. "The voice, together with the look and the whole frame, is responsive to the passions of the mind, as the strings of a musical instrument are to the fingers which touch them. For as a musical instrument has its different keys, so every voice is sharp, full, slow, loud or low: and then each of these keys has different degrees which beget other strains, such as the smooth and the sharp, the contracted and the lengthened, the continued and the interrupted, the tender, the shrill and the swelling.*

4. But the voice, with its wonderful modulations, is unmeasurably aided by THE OTHER PART OF THE ELOQUENCE OF THE BODY. "No man expresses warm and animated feelings with his mouth alone, but with his whole body. He articulates with every limb and joint, and talks from head to foot with a thousand voices."† And how does the accession of fitting gesture to vocal expression emphasize and enhance the latter? In Paul's address to Agrippa, what vivid, overcoming eloquence was added to his vocal utterance, by his dis-

* Cicero.   † Sidney Smith.

playing his chains? "Except these bonds." How did Antony intensify the words of his oration over the dead body of Cæsar, by uncovering it before the eyes of the people, and counting over its wounds one by one? To the peroration of Burke's speech, in the impeachment of Hastings, what an overwhelming force of eloquence was given, when, with streaming eyes and with a suffused countenance, he raised his hands with the documents in them as a testimony to Heaven of the guilt of the person charged?* What had Whitefield's apostrophe "to the attendant angel" been, abstracting from it his *supplosio pedis*, and his lifting up his eyes with gushing tears, compared to what it was by virtue of this accompanying gesticulation? Take from the celebrated conclusion of Webster's argument before the Supreme Court, in the case of Darmouth College, the quivering of the lips, the trembling of the firm cheeks, the choked voice, the eyes overfull of tears, of the great Advocate, and that conclusion would never have been celebrated or remembered.†

* "Never was eloquence more triumphant. His audience could endure the agony no longer. Mrs. Siddons confessed that all the terror and pity she had ever witnessed on the stage, sunk into insignificance before the scene she had just witnessed. Mrs. Sheridan fainted; and the stern Lord Chancellor, Thurlow, who had always in the most headstrong way insisted on Hastings' innocence, was observed for once in his life to shed a tear."

† " The court-room during these two or three minutes, presented an extraordinary spectacle. Chief Justice Marshall bent over as if to catch the slightest whisper; Mr. Justice Washington, at his side, leaning over with an eager troubled look; and the remainder of the court, at the two extremities, pressing as it were to a single point, while the audience were wrapping themselves round

5. **Delivery holds the same place in Preaching, that it has in natural eloquence.** The human in it is not less complete or normal from its subordination to the Divine. The supernatural does but tend to and require perfection in the natural. If therefore delivery is the chief thing in eloquence as such, it is the chief thing in preaching. There are congruities, proprieties of delivery, peculiar to preaching; but they are not in any disagreement with nature; they are, in kind, only such accommodations to occasions and circumstances, as nature requires in different instances and moments of secular oratory. They are but requirements of nature in a peculiar sphere. No eloquence applies more completely and naturally the principles of oratorical art, than the genuine eloquence of the pulpit. *Delivery here also, then, has the supremacy.*

6. There is therefore no justification of the common disparagement of delivery in preaching; and no apology for it. It implies a violation of order beyond a mere violation of nature, a violation of it, also in the sphere of the supernatural—*a counteraction of order in a work in which the chief part belongs to the Holy Spirit: a counteraction of the Spirit's influence and agency in it.* The part which the Spirit has in it, imposes, as its corollary, an obligation on the preacher,

in closer folds beneath the bench, to catch each look and every movement of the speaker's face. If a painter could give us the scene on canvass—their forms and countenances, and Daniel Webster as he then stood in the midst—it would be one of the most touching pictures in the history of eloquence."—*Prof. Goodrich to Mr. Choate.*

to give to delivery his principal regard. Being first in itself, it is first in the regard of the Spirit, who cannot but estimate things as they are. If the preacher puts it last, or aught else above it, he is therein at variance with the Holy Spirit, and impairs if he does not entirely thwart His operation. By the inversion of order for which he makes himself responsible, he cannot but grieve, if he does not altogether quench the Spirit of God. And he will be likely to gain little by misapplying to something else attention which is due to delivery. He will not compose as well, he will not make as good a sermon in any respect, as he would if, in making it, he concurred with the Holy Spirit in his estimation of delivery. Not having been made with just reference to good delivery, it will doubtless be little suitable to it; perhaps incompatible with it; that is to say, as an instrument of oratory, it will be at fault, if not directly opposite to what it should be, in respect to the exigency of eloquence in its chief element. Underrating delivery, therefore, cannot but be inexpedient, in the whole business of preaching. It is a capital mistake and its fruits are after its kind. It is the bane of pulpit eloquence.

7. Proceeding now with our main design, which is to present as far as we can in a few brief remarks, the theory of delivery in preaching, we first of all premise, as its chief principle, that EVEN MORE IF POSSIBLE THAN IN MAKING THE SERMON, THE BUSINESS OF DELIVERING IT, IS SPIRITUAL; CONSISTING IN THE HIGHEST ACTIVITIES OF SPIRITUAL LIFE. Cicero makes

action in speaking radically different from that of the stage: "Orators," he says, "are the *actors* of truth; players but its *mimics*." Infinitely greater is the difference between action in preaching and in other oratory; since the distance is infinite, between nature and spirit.* Just action in speaking, therefore, quite as much as the discourse itself, is of Divine-Human agency. It is impossible to the preacher, except as he is moved and actuated thereto and therein, by the Spirit of God. It is infinitely beyond his ability on two accounts: in the first place, he cannot have the kind of knowledge, the spiritual light and sense necessary to it; and secondly, having this knowledge, he still needs the co-operation of the Spirit, in order to express it appropriately in delivery—*the eloquence of the body*. As to the former, the continued agency of the Spirit is indispensable because spiritual knowledge, unlike the other kind, cannot, from its nature, be retained, or recalled, apart from the unintermitted working of the Holy Ghost in the soul. The preacher may have had the Divine aid in making his sermon; the sermon, both as to its matter and words may be a spiritual one; its delivery nevertheless will not be spiritual, if spiritual knowledge or discernment be required in it; only the *incessant* operation of the Spirit within him, can fulfill this condition.† "I fear," says Pascal, with admirable judgment, "that you do not sufficiently distinguish, between the things you

---

* The infinite distance between body and mind, is a figure of the *infinitely more infinite distance* between mind and love,"— the fruit of the Spirit.—PASCAL. † In a letter to his sister.

speak of (spiritual things) and those of which the world speaks; since it is beyond doubt sufficient to have once learned these latter things, in order to retain them, so as not to require to be taught them again; whereas, it is not sufficient to have once learned those of the other kind, and to have comprehended them in a good way, that is to say, by the internal operation of God, in order to preserve a like knowledge of them, though we may well retain the recollection of them. There is no reason why we should not be able to *remember* them, or why we should not retain in our memory, an epistle of St. Paul as easily as a book of Virgil. But the knowledge which we acquire in this way, as well as the continuation of it, is but an effect of memory; whereas in order that those who are of heaven may understand this secret and strange language, it is needful that the same grace which alone can give the first understanding of it should *continue it, and render it always present, by graving it incessantly in the hearts of the faithful, so as to keep it always alive.* As in the blessed, God is continually renewing their beatitude which is an effect and consequence of grace; as also the church holds, that the Father continually produces the Son, and maintains the eternity of His being, by an effusion of His own substance, which is without interruption as well as without end." But in a spiritual delivery, the continued influence of the Spirit, is on another account required; spiritual knowledge, its indispensable condition is not sufficient for it of itself. It cannot express itself in the appropriate action, without being aided therein by the Spirit: it is not provided for by knowledge alone. Action, which is more than knowledge, needs aid for itself. In elocutionary action, as well as in thinking and writing, the preacher, however qualified by self culture, can attain to no degree of spirituality, by merely natural effort. If the activity of a preacher in speaking, the eloquence of the body, be indeed spiritual, it is doubtless a higher exercise of the spiritual life, than either of its other exercises in the business of preaching. It must needs be so, if it be answerable, in all respects, to the unique and mysterious exigencies of such a work, as delivering appropriately the inspired word of God as a vehicle and representative of the Holy Spirit. Apart from a very special operation of the Spirit himself, who is sufficient for the just performance of this work?—spiritual things, expressing themselves fitly, in spiritual modulations of the voice, spiritual looks, spiritual attitudes—the supernatural exerting itself proportionately in and through these bodily signs of thought and feeling—think of one's having in himself, an independent sufficiency for this! The apostles, with all their gifts for other uses, had it not, nay, even our Lord's spirituality of mind and knowledge, added to the perfectly natural use of the human powers did not qualify Him adequately, for the business of dispensing the word, independently of the continued co-agency of the Spirit in this specific business; even He delivered His discourses, under the anointing and in the power of the Spirit of God.*

* Luke iv. 18, cf. 21, iv. 14.

After His resurrection, it was still, through the Holy Ghost, that He gave commandment to the apostles whom He had chosen.*

8. It need hardly be added, that IN ALL PRELIMINARY WORK WITH REFERENCE TO DELIVERY, THE PREACHER MUST ABIDE IN COMMUNION WITH THE HOLY SPIRIT. He is not sufficient, of himself, for the least of the exercises of self-culture prerequisite to just pulpit action. The teachers of elocution, with their utmost assiduities, cannot make him independent of the Spirit's aid in practising aright the rules of art, relative to delivery in preaching, or in studying aright the philosophy of voice and gesture. They cannot instruct him, in what he chiefly needs to know and do, in order to act well his part in pronouncing his discourses. No appliances, whether simply natural or artistic, can effect anything to this end of themselves; they may suffice for the orators of the world; they come infinitely short of meeting the necessities of preachers. As far as preparatory practice for pulpit delivery proceeds, on the contrary supposition its failure is inevitable. It is so of necessity; were it otherwise, it might become so by real, if not conscious visitations of Divine displeasure. It is an offence, a glaring disrespect to the Holy Spirit whose proffered aid it declines. Let not the ministers of the Word forget for a moment the most intimate and sacred relations—relations never for a moment suspended—between the work of their office and the high prerogatives of the Holy Spirit in the economy of the Gospel.

* Acts i. 2.

9. In regard to PARTICULAR POINTS OF ATTENTION, THE DETAILS OF APPLICATION IN CULTIVATING DELIVERY, there is no substantial difference between preaching and other kinds of public eloquence. Preachers cannot be too well acquainted with the theory of elocution; cannot know too well the principles of emphasis, the science of the passions, and their interrelations with each other; how they naturally express themselves in the tones of the voice, the looks, attitudes, movements of the body, etc.* The spirituality of pulpit action, and the part in it belonging to the Holy Ghost, interfere in no degree with the highest culture in reference to it. On the contrary, they favor and promote it. It is one of the proper designs of the Spirit's influence to secure attention to it as far as possible. It is among the ends to which He lends His aid; and it is not to be doubted that the general neglect so much to be deplored, into which delivery in preaching has fallen, is to be ascribed, in great measure, to want of pains-taking with regard to it arising from being out of the Spirit's counsel in this matter. It is not of Him that preachers have been inclined to neglect the scientific study of elocution. The labor which this study requires is, doubtless, the explanation of its being neglected. The labor unquestionably, is a severe one; but had the Holy Spirit been obeyed, it would have been accepted as a pleasure.†

* See Cicero, de Oratore, lib. iii. c. 56-61.
† Labor ipse voluptas—when performed in the strength of the Spirit.

10. But supposing that no preliminary pains have been omitted, and that nothing remains but delivery itself, WHAT METHOD SHOULD BE FOLLOWED IN THIS PART OF PREACHING? The actual methods are three: *Reading, Reciting* and *Extemporising*. Reserving the last for the moment, which of the first two should be preferred? Both reproduce a written discourse, which does it in the better manner? Taking them in their best form, Reciting, doubtless, has the advantage. In general, reciting is injured by requiring an effort of memory in order to recall the words of the discourse. But there is a kind of recitation which has no such inconvenience; the reciter, in this case, has no more concern about his words or linguistic forms than the extemporizer; he uses the very expressions he has written; but he does this from his perfect possession of his subject, not from a consciously distinct exercise of recollection. He has his composition so exactly and thoroughly *by heart*, that to reproduce it he has but to open his mouth; his utterance of it is as spontaneous as his breathing. We speak what to us is a mystery, but we are acquainted with an eminent person, in whom, according to his own assertion to us, it is actualized. His language in speaking, though, elaborately written, is as spontaneous as it would be if he were extemporizing. So intimately identified and united are his thought and the form of it in his manuscript, that it would require an effort to separate them. Such a way of reciting as this, is, undoubtedly, preferable to the best way of reading. But it is very uncommon; except to a few privileged geniuses, it is

extremely difficult if not impossible. To almost every one who practices it, reciting is a labor of recollection, requiring even for an imperfect performance of it, an anxious mental application. This fact is a very grave objection to this method being generally adopted. For by how much the mind is occupied in recalling forms of expression, by so much is it disabled for the work itself of delivery. This is no part of the business; it is another business; the common reciter attempts two things at once. He puts himself to an impracticable task; his delivery is bad at best; and, what is another serious disadvantage, he is apt to betray a solicitude, lest the words of his manuscript escape him; and the hearers perceiving his embarrassment, are hindered from attending to what he says, by sympathetic trouble, fearing that his memory may fail him. Generally, therefore, reciting is much inferior to reading, at least to the best way of reading. It is inferior, we think, to reading as commonly practiced. Bad as this is, there is no interference in it from a distinct exercise of thought about another matter, and whether interested by it or not, the hearers are at ease.

11. DELIVERY BY READING MAY RISE TO HIGH EXCELLENCE.—In this method one may be exclusively occupied by the sense; the words are before his eye; but he does not think of them; he is not conscious of seeing them; the subject with reference to its purpose wholly engrosses him; he has no concern except through reading, to possess his hearers of it, and compel them to yield to its force. Into his delivery, such

as it is, he throws himself entirely; his action may be very defective; his gestures, especially, may be awkward or ungraceful; but his hearers are so interested with what he says, that they see nothing amiss. Infinitely different is reading like this from ordinary reading, which simply reports what is written on the page. This reading does more than inform; it is full of living fire; it conveys the preacher's soul, all aglow with the inspiration of his subject, and the purpose for which he treats it. Such was the method of Chalmers, the most eloquent preacher of his age. He read, but what was his reading as an instrument of oratory! Edwards, too, was a reader—a quiet reader—but in what demonstration of the Spirit and power was the preaching of that great man of God!

12. But neither in Reciting nor in Reading DOES THE IDEAL OF DELIVERY RESIDE. As to reading, the best of these methods, a very high authority would hardly admit it into a comparison with that which we named last. "Pleadings which are read," says Pliny,* "lose all their force and warmth and well nigh their very name, as being things which the gestures of the speaker, his bold advances, even his changes of position and the activity of his body, in harmony with all the emotions of the mind, are wont at once to enforce and kindle. But the eyes and hands of one who reads, which are the main auxiliaries of delivery, are fettered, so that it is no wonder the attention of the auditors flags, since it is sustained by no charm, and awakened by no excitement from

* Epist. IV: lib. ii.

without." Edwards, also, notwithstanding his contrary practice, which, in the latter part of his life, he thought it had been well had he never followed, pronounced delivery without notes the most natural way, and that which had the greatest tendency, on the whole, to answer the end of preaching. It appeared evident to him, to have been the manner of the apostles and primitive ministers of the Gospel.* A thousand examples demonstrate the incomparable superiority of this manner. By the side of that of Whitefield, what is the best possible way of reading! In his looks; his tears; the flashes, glances, suffusion of his eyes; in his attitudes and changes of position; in the sudden effects of reaction on himself from observed impressions on the hearers, what matchless eloquence—utterly impossible in any other than extemporaneous speaking! Admitting that it was spiritual as well as natural, as it doubtless may have been and was in a high degree, the conclusion is intuitive, that delivery can rise into its highest sphere only in extemporaneous discourse. Think of the spiritual and the natural combining harmoniously in such an instance of the eloquence of the body as the following: "Treating of the sufferings of our Saviour, as though Gethsemane were in sight, he would say—stretching out his hand: 'Look yonder—What is it I see? It is my agonizing Lord.' And as though it were no difficult matter to catch the sound of our Lord praying, he would exclaim: 'Hark! hark! do you not hear Him?'" Wonderful preaching! We admit that it is of the

---

* Life of Edwards, by Dr. Hopkins.

best in its kind; but we are contrasting with it the very best of any other.

13. We go on to say that IT IS AGAINST TRUE ART, AGAINST NATURE, AND, OF COURSE, AGAINST THE DOMINION OF THE HOLY SPIRIT, IN DELIVERY, TO PUT AMONG PREPARATIVES FOR IT A PRESCRIBED OR PREMEDITATED SCHEME FOR REGULATING IT; to determine beforehand what the emphases, looks, gestures, are to be in particular parts, and perhaps to preactualize them in a rehearsal "practiced at the glass." On two accounts, this must be a preposterous way. In the first place, just action in speaking cannot be anticipated: the time for it must indicate it. It is only the critical moment itself that can give its idea; it is contingent on the unimaginable futuritions and incidents of elocution. But were it otherwise, good delivery after this method would be an impossibility. With a programme of action artistically perfect, the speaker would have no advantage; he could not carry it out justly. He could make no good use of it. The very attempt to use it would disable him for proper elocution. What art could conceal the art he would be trying to practice? and what effect on his delivery, from the labor to conceal it? The hearers doubtless would not fail to know; itself the surest testimony to its absurdity. As to all earnest action having an object ulterior to itself, it is an instinct of nature, that not its *manner* but its *object;* or, in such a business as that of public speaking, its subject with reference to its object, be exclusively regarded at the moment of performing it. Even a good reader obeys this instinct. "A reader is

sure to pay too much attention to his voice, not only if he pays any at all, but if he does not strenuously labor* to withdraw his attention from it altogether. He who not only understands fully what he is reading, but is earnestly occupying his mind with the matter of it, would be likely to read as if he understood it. And in like manner, with a view to the *impressiveness* of the delivery, he who not only feels it but is exclusively absorbed with that feeling, will be likely to read as if he felt it, and to communicate the impression to his hearers. But this cannot be the case if he is occupied with the thought of what their opinion will be of his reading, and *how his voice ought to be regulated;* if, in short, he is thinking of himself, and, of course, in the same degree abstracting his attention from that which ought to occupy it exclusively."† It is therefore certain that there should be no labor in speaking to carry out a scheme of delivery. The study of delivery, now, must be forborne; proper application to this study is *previous*, like the educational training by which one is furnished for artistic action in all particular art performances. One who applies the principles of art (*e.g.*), in writing or in playing of an instrument of music, gives while doing this no direct thought to these principles; they have become a second nature to him, through his familiarity with them. Scarcely more does the bee act by instinct in building its cell according to

---

* In order to overcome a contrariant inclination, too wont to be besetting him.

† Whately.

the principles of mechanics, than he does in his exquisite exemplifications of art. So acts the accomplished speaker in delivering his discourse. He has studied delivery; but he is not studying it now. He knows the theory of delivery; this has acquainted him with his old faults in speaking. He has corrected them; he has formed good elocutionary habits. Hence, and hence alone, his security for proper action on occasions as they arise.

14. In accordance with this principle of Delivery, VERY EMINENT PROFICIENTS IN IT HAVE PROTESTED STRONGLY AGAINST ALL ATTEMPTS TO FOLLOW OUT A FORCASTED PROGRAMME OF ACTION. The great tragedian of the recent past,* after experience of the disadvantages of this method, gives his testimony concerning it, in these striking terms: "It has been imagined, even by enlightened minds, that in studying my parts I place myself before a glass, as a model before a painter in his *atelier*. According to them, I gesticulate, I shake the ceiling of the room with my cries. In the evening on the stage, I utter the intonations I learned in the morning: prepared inflections and sobs of which I know the number; imitating Crecentini, who, in his Romeo, evinces a despair beforehand, in a passage sung a hundred times over at home, with a piano accompaniment. It is an error. *Reflection* is one of the greatest parts of my labor. Following the example of the poet, I walk, I muse, or even seat myself on the margin of my little river: like the poet, I rub my forehead; it is the only gesture I allow myself; and you

* Talma.

know it is by no means one of the grandest. Oh, how a thing becoming historical remains true! If any one should inquire how I have found the greater part of my greatest successes, I should reply, by *constantly thinking of them*. We were rhetoricians and not dramatic personages. How many academic discourses on the stage! How few words of simplicity! But one evening chance threw me into the parlor with the leaders of the Gironde Party; their sombre and disquieted appearance attracted my attention. There were written there, in visible characters, great and mighty interests. As they were too much men of heart to allow these interests to be tainted with selfishness, I saw there manifest proofs of the danger of the country. All were assembled for pleasure, yet no one thought of it. Discussion ensued; they touched the most thrilling questions of the crisis. It was beautiful: I imagined myself present at a secret deliberation of the Roman Senate. It is thus, thought I, that men should *speak*. The country, whether it be named France or Rome, employs the same accents, the same language. If they do not *declaim* here, neither did they declaim in the olden time, it is evident. These reflections made me more attentive. My impressions, though produced by a conversation void of all *emphase*, became profound. An apparent calmness in these men, thought I, agitates the soul. Eloquence then may have force without throwing the body into disorderly movements. I even perceived that discourse uttered without effort or outcry, renders the gesture more energetic, and gives more expression to the countenance. All these deputies, thus assembled before me, appeared far more eloquent than at the *tribune*, where, finding themselves a spectacle, they thought it necessary to utter their harangues in the manner of actors as we then were ; that is to say, of *declaimers* fraught with turgidity. *From that moment I caught new light, and saw my art regenerated.*"

15. After proper self-culture in elocution and renewing the prerequisite communion with the Holy Spirit, the only condition of success, the only object of preliminary concern, in a particular instance of preaching, IS TO BE FULLY POSSESSED, TO BE THOROUGHLY INSPIRED BY THE SUBJECT AND THE OCCASION. This is the prime necessity of all eloquence ; it was the discovery of the great French actor, when his eyes were opened to see the true secret of delivery. Hence it was that *reflection* became his great labor; that he walked, mused, sat on the margin of the river, rubbed his forehead after the manner of the poet. He sought to absorb himself in his subject ; he left action to itself. Being qualified generally for his art, by acquainting himself with the philosophy of the voice and of gesture, and by just self-culture, in accordance with it, he assumed that what remained to him, as the prerequisite of success, was to get perfect command of his subject; or, to speak better, to give the subject perfect command and supremacy over him. This, with the qualifications just mentioned, is all that remains to the preacher ; and his is no other than the player's way of gaining it. That way is the thorough rumination of the subject, meditating on it over and over again ;

not the committing to memory the words he is to repeat, with premeditated action, but the working their meaning, their strength, into himself; the filling himself with their total sense; the vitalizing himself with it in its breadth, length, depth and height; the making it so live and rule in all his life, that its procession from him in delivery shall be rather a spontaneous outflow than the result of a separate memoriter effort. Doubtless, the memory is exercised, intensely exercised, even when this is done; but not exclusively or distinguishably to the consciousness from the other powers of the mind. The memory and these are united, are inter-blended in the operation, as rays in the sunbeam. There may be moments when it acts by itself, even in a delivery very good on the whole; but they are exceptive and anxious moments; and the delivery now deteriorates, and witnesses against itself as violating its norm. As soon as the recollective faculty is distinctively exercised, the speaker generally betrays the fact; his hearers see his hesitation, and begin to tremble for him lest his memory should lapse, and to wish he had his manuscript lying open before him.

16. IT IS IMPOSSIBLE TO PRESCRIBE A STANDARD OF ACTION FOR ALL PREACHERS. There are peculiar congruities of pulpit delivery which must not be violated; the preacher with his hearers is in the temple; he is the representative of the awful presence of God; on matters of infinite moment he acts in the name of the great and dreadful *Unseen*. The difference as to interest between his business and that of any orator of the

world, makes the latter, however great in itself, less than nothing comparatively. Without being under a total eclipse of spiritual illumination, and entirely out of the communion and harmony with the Holy Ghost, he cannot be insensible to this fact; and if he has but a faint impression of it, he cannot allow himself in certain modes and ways of action, which, in secular orators, are sometimes proper and even highly admirable; they would be unnatural, monstrous, in the elocution of the pulpit. Nevertheless, who may give the preacher an absolute rule or criterion of delivery? Beyond self-evident, palpable improprieties, every preacher is a rule to himself; his idiosyncrasy is his rule. What would be a just measure to one, would be a defective or an extremely excessive and absurd one to another. The lion does not more differ from the lamb, than preachers from one another in elocutionary gifts. In different preachers, vehemence and gentleness, commotion and stillness, thunder and whisper, whirlwind and zephyr, are both alike appropriate characteristics; as they are also very suitable and natural, in the same preachers at different moments. Both, too, are alike acceptable to the Spirit, who attempers His influences to the natures of His instruments, making them now as the softest breath, now as a rushing mighty wind, or as lightning and fire. It is not by the quantity, but by the quality of pulpit action that the holy proprieties are on the one hand violated, and on the other maintained. There may be the sublimest form of spirituality in abundant and stormy action; and there may be nothing better than the affectation of tenderness, in a quiet, soft, reserved manner of delivery.*

17. It follows from what we have just been saying, or rather is included in it, that IMITATION CAN HAVE NO PLACE IN JUST ACTION IN SPEAKING. In this as well as in invention, in disposition, in the entire construction and finish of his discourse, a true speaker is himself and not another; he is generally true even to his habitual imperfections of manner. Without renouncing his own identity he may profit by observing excellencies and faults in the elocution of others; he may thus acquaint himself better with his own defects, instruct himself better generally in the regulation of his voice, emphasis, attitudes, etc.; and stimu-

---

* How far violent or very demonstrative action may have place in preaching without indecorum, no rule can determine. Whitefield was often exceedingly demonstrative, but so far as we know, never undignified or ungraceful. The severest criticism, that of Hume, Chesterfield, Franklin, Garrick, gave it transcendent praise. How vehement was the delivery of Chalmers! how terrible that of Knox! how lion-like that of Luther! Each a mighty man of God, a chosen and an eminent vehicle of the power of the Holy Ghost. We once heard a sermon from the elder Mason, the delivery of which combined, with unexceptionable propriety, a manner in the highest degree bold and even dramatic. He began with a rap on the desk, personating one knocking at the door—"a messenger from the world of spirits." He used personation freely in the midst of the discourse, and at the close, it rose to sublimity. The subject was—*deliverance from bondage through the fear of death.* (Heb. ii. 15.) He first *dramatized* the death-bed scene of one who died in his sins—a wilful neglecter of this great salvation; and then that of a triumphant believer. His manner was to the last in keeping with its surprising outset. We had no sense of anything at all amiss in this wonderful instance of pulpit elocution. It seemed to be no less proper than unusual.

late himself in studying the principles and philosophy of delivery; but he could not but mar his own action by endeavoring to model it after another's. He might as soon change himself into another man as be natural any longer. If his hearers happen to be acquainted with the example he is striving to copy, they will not fail to see his weakness, and—what of itself sufficiently confutes all such imitation—they cannot but think it unfortunate for him; a palpable vanity. A tolerable speaker he might perhaps have been if he had been content with himself; he has made himself an intolerable one by his pitiable emulation. It remains that after studying models with reference to general improvement, the only thing in which they are to be imitated is that by which they made themselves models, namely, their absolute independence and forgetfulness of models in delivery.

18. It seems to us that one of the chief causes of bad delivery in preaching, a sufficient cause of it, certainly, is THE CHARACTER OF THE ORDINARY SERMON, SO CALLED, ESPECIALLY ITS DEFECT IN RESPECT OF THE ORATORICAL ELEMENT, THE BUSINESS-LIKE CHARACTER OF ALL TRUE ORATORY. Delivery in discourse takes its stamp, in part, from the sort of discourse which is given; oratorical delivery requires an *oration;* that is to say, a discourse which is an *affair,* an earnest, agonistic speech, which has a single point ulterior to itself, and which has no other concern than to carry that point. Preaching is too seldom discourse like this. It is sometimes chiefly expository, as perhaps it should be. But when preaching is not of this form,

when it uses what has the name of *the sermon*, which, by its etymology should be *an oration par excellence*,* it is frequently, if not generally, as a whole, no oration at all: it has several points instead of one; perhaps indeed no point in particular. It treats several co-ordinate propositions; it is rather an analysis than a synthetic speech, like that of a pleader at the bar; it makes a treatise or an essay: it is without oratorical unity; of course, it cannot but be defective in oratorical delivery: and if such be the actual character of preaching, as undoubtedly it is to a great extent, this defect is but its natural and proper concomitant. Nor is there a possibility of the desired change in the elocution of the pulpit, while preaching retains this abnormal character. It surely ought not to retain it as extensively as it has done. Preaching in its ideal is a species of oratory; the noblest form of it. In its ordinary efforts no discourse should excel it in singleness of design, or in strenuous, suasory, synthetic urgency to attain its end. In some of its specimens (those *e. g.* of Baxter, Edwards, Chalmers), no discourse, not that of Demosthenes or Burke, does in these respects excel it. Let preaching be generally true to its own idea, its supreme law as a means to the highest of all ends, and with just cultivation of delivery, preachers, in respect to this part of eloquence, will cease to hide their "diminished heads" in the presence of other speakers. At least, it is only on

---

* Why, else, should the term *sermon* (speech), be restricted to sacred discourse, as if a secular oration was, comparatively, not a *speech* at all?

this condition that even with the utmost attention to delivery, much proficiency in it is to be expected. The character of the discourse will continue to overrule and determine that of its delivery, in conformity to itself.

19. There is, let us add, a conventional restraint on pulpit elocution, *from the preacher's place in the assembly*. He stands above and at a distance from them, behind a desk, which conceals more than half his person. His seclusion may give him some conveniences in conducting the immediate preliminaries of preaching; but it should be no privilege to him in delivering his discourse. If an earnest speaker "articulates with every limb and joint, and talks from head to foot, with a thousand voices," how much is an earnest preacher curtailed of his means of bodily expression, by the narrow enclosure which he occupies? He is without advantage from his lower limbs; his bust only is seen; he cannot change his position; his attitudes are but half visible, and for this cause, probably, disagreeable. How must his delivery be marred by these subtractions of "the eloquence of the body?" Compare with it that of a speaker who stands fully in view, and presents in his entire person, a complete, graceful example of this crowning glory of oratory. That preachers, exclusively, should be thus restricted in elocution is but a prescription of arbitrary tradition : nothing in the peculiarity of spiritual eloquence requires it; it maims this noblest of all eloquences; it presupposes a theory of preaching, which makes delivery in it a thing of little or no moment; it has

doubtless had no small influence in reducing it to this estimation, in the general practice, if not also in the opinion of the pulpit. If in the pulpit of the future, delivery is to assume its rightful supremacy, tradition, in this matter, will dominate no longer; the principles of true art, which are, at last, but the principles of simple nature, will assert their authority; and preaching, like speaking in the forum or the senate, will be free of all such abridgments of elocutionary force as tradition has so unwarrantably prescribed to it.

20. IS IT TO BE EXPECTED THAT THE REFORM WILL ACTUALLY HAVE PLACE? A change in the form of preaching is doubtless at hand. The renovating power which has been changing all things in science, in art, in the physical, social and civil life of man, cannot but be felt, indeed has manifestly been felt, by the modern pulpit. Already preaching, as to form, is, in several respects, different from what it has ever been. In some respects we think it is better. It is by no means changed as much as it should be. It ought to be in advance of the other instruments of change which are exerting themselves with such astonishing efficiency in every sphere of human life. There is no object of deeper interest to every true philanthropist, every one who identifies the progress of humanity with the success of the gospel, than that preaching should receive a new and healthful impulse, which shall give it the precedence to which it is entitled,—a just adaptation to humanity in its present excited and over-active state, and a regulating power of all the changes which

with such unparalleled rapidity are coming to pass everywhere in the world. But it is as yet very far from having this pre-eminence of control. There is an imperative demand for further variance, we might almost say a revolution in the form of it. And is not this demand to be met? In that Future of overwhelming interest, which all men feel to be just before us, which indeed is now opening itself upon us and inspiring us with wonder at what is surely and swiftly coming, what will preaching be, if accommodated, as it should and must be if it is to play well its part—to the unparalleled circumstances in which it will find itself? Imperfect as our anticipation of them must be, we cannot but be sure in general, from signs before us, that they will be circumstances of earnest, intense materialism, of an exceedingly practical, matter-of-fact bearing, such as have not been dreamt of in all the past; causes are already in operation before our eyes, which make the anticipation of this almost as reality itself. Surely amidst such circumstances, preaching, if true to its mission, will not take from the present or any former period, its measures or its methods of practice. There must be, in these respects, a novelty in it, parallel, or, when need be, antithetic to the novelty of its unexampled surroundings. Its character cannot be precisely foreseen; it will be, we would hope, as didactic, as discriminative, as solid, in all respects as scholarly, as it has been at any time ; we cannot but hope it will be so from necessities which will be upon it, and from its present advantages of culture. But how changed must it be, especially in its chief performances, in respect of oratorical freedom, force and action? It cannot but be, pre-eminently, it would seem, of *the nature of business*—" business which is a business :"* It will still treat " subjects ;" but it will need to treat them, not as terminating in themselves, or in the way of analysis or disquisition, but with reference to issues or specific ends: to determine first, not on either texts or subjects, but on points to be carried, on things to be done ; and, as in all earnest oratory, to be, in all its propositions, enlargements, utterances, ornaments, but a strenuous means of attaining definite ends : to strive, of course, to avail itself of the advantages of just delivery, the peerless eloquence of appropriate action. This, its chief means, it may no longer forego or neglect. Due attention to delivery, and due provision for it, will be a deeply felt necessity. It will suffer no traditional trammels ; it will follow out the inviolable principles of eloquence ; it will obey nature and the free Spirit of God. If it meet the high exigencies of the epoch, it cannot take the word of command from tradition, or the perfunctory examples of these or former times.

* Preacher, your business is a *business ;* yet more than Senators and Advocates, you are Advocates and Senators : Be both. Let your pulpits be to you alternately a tribune and a bar ; let your word be *an action directed to an immediate object :* Let not your hearers come to hear a discourse, so much as to receive a message. Possess yourselves, possess them, of all the *advantages,* which pertain to the subjects of the pulpit. Your eloquence has more artless aspects, and more vivid tints, than that of the Senate or the Bar ; nothing condemns it to abstraction ; *everything impels it toward sensible facts.*"—Vinet, p. 503.

21. But will the change after all have place? Will delivery in the preaching of the all-pregnant future, whose dawn is already advancing, have its rightful pre-eminence? Will this form of preaching, which cannot but be new, be what it should be, in this grand respect? Or will the construction of the sermon continue to be the all-absorbing concern of preachers and its delivery comparatively as nothing? We cannot confidently say. The undervaluation of delivery at the present moment, and too generally in foregoing times, in view of its inherent unjustness and the standing reprobation of it by the reason of things and the verdict of the human mind, begets hesitation as to the probability of a correction of it, under the influence of any possible circumstances; and yet since it has pleased God to institute preaching as the leading instrumentality, the means of means, in applying his efficacious grace, must not "the wickedness of the wicked" rush on to its climax and its doom, if the correction shall not take place? In a practice of preaching so wrong, so utterly ineloquent, in the thing of chief moment, as that now generally prevailing, will the Spirit of God who can give no sanction to inherent impropriety of any sort, work with that plentitude of His power, which will be necessary to write "holiness to the Lord," on such inventions and aboundings of secular life, as those which we already see in such rapid progress must become in their culmination? As, then, no change is to be expected in God's plan for reducing men to obedience to Himself, must not the change we are speaking of in preaching be a reality

at length, if the triumph of the gospel on earth is to be a reality?

22. And WHY SHOULD IT NOT BE INAUGURATED AT ONCE? The very occasion for it presupposes a high existing culpability in the ministers of the word. No tongue can express the evil of delivering Christian truths *as if they were fictions*. As far as preachers are chargeable with this evil, they have cause for the deepest humiliation. Next to counting Christ Himself a myth, nay identical with it in effect, is so representing His doctrine. What infidelity whether in itself or in its consequences is worse? We know it is pleading for a paradox to insist on the reform, as an immediate necessity; but if a paradox be true and the truth important, these facts imply criminality in its being a paradox,* and imperatively require that it be so no longer. Think of it as we may, the prevailing way of delivery, in preaching, is matter for the profoundest regret to the ministry and the church. Whether it is to remain in the coming times or not, it should, for the sake of the times now present, from henceforth cease, or cease to be excused or tolerated. Infinite interests demand that the reform begin without delay.

23. LET NOT THE CHANGE SEEM IMPRACTICABLE. No circumstances, no powers of argument or persuasion, can of themselves effect it; these can produce no spiritual fruit whatever; and this, as we have seen, is the highest perfection of this kind of fruit; but there is on this account no cause for discouragement. The power to be ultimately relied on, in the whole business

---

* Paradox—Something against prevailing opinion.

of preaching, is the power of the Holy Ghost. It is the privilege, it is the duty, of preachers, to be full of the Holy Ghost, and workers together with Him in every part of their labor. The chief thing, the only thing virtually necessary to the change, is what they cannot be wanting in, without sinning alike against themselves and against the highest law of their function, the law of all its laws. Remembering the Divine-Human character of preaching, let them rise above themselves, as they should and may without presumption, into the illuminations and sanctities of the Eternal Spirit; and over all difficulties connected with the cultivation and practice of just delivery in preaching they will be already triumphant. And if they live to be preachers in the opening Future they will pass into it prepared for its eventful activities and developments; and whether they live or die, under the consciousness of their new impulses and experiences, they will well fulfill what remains of their sacred mission; and for that part of it, at least, be able to endure the fiery ordeal through which every preacher's work, with himself, will have to pass in the judgment of the great day of the Lord.

IX.

FRAGMENTS OF THOUGHT.

I.—OPTIMISM.

If there be several courses of action claiming our choice, some better than others, and one best of all, goodness obliges us to prefer this last to all the others; goodness were otherwise disowned, in so far as it stands in the best above what it does in the better and the simply good—for all that is goodness which differences the good from the best. Here, in brief, is the demonstration of Optimism. Optimism is true, if goodness may not be disallowed; if the difference may not pass for nothing between good, better, and best.

It may be that a better than either of the solicitors of choice is a negation of them all; doing nothing, letting the several courses remain ideal only, may be better than to actualize the best of them, which, in that case, were to obey the behest of Optimism. Absolute quietism, the latency of power, would then be the expression of Optimism.

Applying this to the Deity, the existence of the world is proof that Optimism did not demand the inertia or latency of creative power. The rule of the best required this power to reveal itself in an actual creation. A world was a necessity, if Optimism was to be determinative. God would not have realized His own idea, or done what seemed to Him best, had He not given existence to a creation external to Himself.

And the same principle of necessity required that the creation be that which came into being—that, and not another. He could not have given existence to another without disowning goodness, for goodness, in His idea, stood in this creation above itself in any other; there was no ideal creation, different from this that seemed to Him so good. The existing world, therefore, and not another must have been created. This world was a moral necessity.

And as with its creation, so likewise with its economy or government—the rule of the best could not but obtain. Among conceivable economies different from one another, as to goodness, the perfection and blessedness of the Deity required Him to take the best. The All-Perfect, whose moral essence is pure goodness, could have been content with no other.

Since, therefore, evil exists, the best world, under the best government, was one in which this was possible; and Optimism, the antitheton of evil, consists with this possibility. But the possibility of evil is not its reality; there may be a prevention of the latter, though the former may have place. And goodness self-evidently demands its prevention, if this be possible. This is true; still, the preventive agency, as much as the creative and controlling, must abide under the sway of Optimism. That only which is best may be done to prevent the appearance of evil. The possibility of preventing it, therefore, is thus conditioned. It cannot be prevented without offending against goodness, if it be not preventable by the best agency that can be employed for the purpose. There is a good, a better, and a best, in conceivable agencies, in this case; the idea of the best was in the mind of the Deity. He could have given reality to no other idea. Evil is not to be prevented, indeed is not preventable, by a violation of the principle of Optimism. That, itself, were greater evil, virtually, than the evil it would prevent; it would undeify God.

The same necessity, the dominion of the best, holds as to the remedy or removal of evil. If there had been in the Divine Mind, a kind or plan of agency better than that which God has employed, it would have taken the place of this. If the direct intervention of physical power, or arbitrary volition, or aught else, had been better, this would not have been preferred; Optimism would have prevailed here, also: the remedy, otherwise, would have been worse, virtually, than the evil.

Optimism, then, the law, the prevalence of the Best, is the principle of the Divine goodness in the Universe. Nothing asserts its own truth with higher evidence than this proposition. To deny it, is to set goodness against itself; to deny it, when its terms are understood, would seem to imply an intention to affirm a contradiction.

In connection with the above, it is edifying to note some results of other applications of the doctrine of Optimism.

It condemns wishing that the world did not exist. Among human wishes, two have been not a little prominent: that there were no Creation, and that there were no God. Both would abolish goodness—the former the realization of the ideal of finite goodness; the latter, Infinite goodness itself. Let the reasons for these wishes be recalled; in what reproach do they implicate their authors!

Again, it challenges, in God's behalf, the highest praise of His creatures. It assures them that the best of worlds exists under the best of administrations, and the best agencies for preventing and remedying evil. How urgent the demand for praise, such as that which is made in the last three of the Psalms! and how unworthy and unhappy the spirit of those who refuse to meet this demand!

Once more: it is the absolute reprobation of sin. It is, by its name, the opposite of evil. It is the doctrine of the preference of the greatest good which sin would destroy. It announces that when a world was to be created, the best of all worlds was determined on; the same preference of the best in establishing a government over the world; the same in preventing, and the same in remedying evil. Let men believe and obey Optimism, and they could bear no sin in themselves, and omit to use no proper means in expelling it from the world. Applied to human life, Optimism is the same as in other applications of it. It requires men to adopt the best plan of life, to do all the good possible to them, and to improve perfectly all their powers, opportunities and means in diffusing good.

II.—THE DIVINE PURPOSES.

The purposes of the Divine mind, though without succession in time, have a relation to each other to which the order of their fulfilment correlates and agrees. And as events have their reason or justification in the order in which they occur, so have the Divine Purposes theirs, in their order or relation to each other. The particular purposes which eventuated in the exercises of creative power, depended on the prime purpose to create; those which the scheme of redemption fulfilled, depended on the purpose to redeem; and the particular purposes themselves were also interdependent, requiring and required by one another. It is impossible for us to comprehend a Timeless order or relation; but as a reality it is not less certain to us than the existence of the Deity, to whom, as infinite or eternal, time, with its successions and changes, is wholly and necessarily objective or extrinsic. The inward activities of the Divine Nature are eternally immanent; but its very idea, as all perfect, requires that there be in these activities an absolutely perfect order; and to suppose that any one of them may have no reference or relation to any or every other, is to make the Supreme Being GOD no longer.

Proper regard to the fact of TIMELESS order or

inter-relation, in the Purposes of God, is indispensable to all just thinking concerning the relation between these Purposes and the Divine ways or conduct. The ways of God pertain to the sphere of time or the finite; His purposes exist in the infinite, or are timeless. If the latter fact be not kept in mind,—if the Divine Purposes and the Divine Ways are regarded as in the same category as to time,—the same predications will be made of both, the distinction, in statement and discourse, between the finite and the infinite, will be lost, and nothing but the finite will remain. The Divine Mind will be conceived of as but a magnified human one, having a like beginning and ending, a like fore and after, a like capacity of growth and decrease, in its inherent activity, with the mind of man;—with no other difference than that of enlargement to an indefinite extent. Thus eternity becomes but a longer time; the infinite but a multitude of finites; and the world, in its vicissitudes, an exponent of purposes, springing up and disappearing, in the mind of its Maker, one after another, in time, according to the Time-order which has place in the course of events. Whence,—since time, in the purpose, must antecede it in events,—a Fatalism, in all things, destructive of the foundations of piety and virtue, and implying that there is, in truth, no such Being as an infinite and good God. It is incidental to the imperfections of human language, that in speaking of events, and the Divine Purposes, in their connection with one another, we sometimes apply terms to the latter which are strictly appropriate only to temporal things; but such anthropomorphisms must be carefully excluded when we would make precise statements of truth concerning the Nature of the Deity; otherwise we shall make the Eternal and the Infinite altogether such a one as ourselves.*

Let then the Ways of God, or events, be thought of as they are, and in the proper sphere. If now they commend themselves to right reason, when we pass to the Divine Purposes, of which they are the development, we shall find nothing here to vary their character, since this is the sphere of the infinite or timeless, in which there is no succession, no fore nor after, nothing to come into thought except the Divine Purposes themselves as existing in their eternal relations to one another. Of these purposes, with their interrelations, the Divine ways are the expression. If, as thus expressed, they cannot be objected to, there is no ground of objection to them. The ways of God are justified, and equally so are His purposes. The justification of the former is the justification of both. If, in all places of His dominion, the works of God praise Him, so likewise do His purposes, of which His works are the execution.

The principle of identity, as to their justification,

---

* An infinite length of Time, distinguished by successive parts, properly and truly so, or a succession of limited and unmeasurable periods of Time, following one another in an infinitely long series, must needs be a groundless imagination. The eternity of God's existence is nothing else but his immediate, perfect, and invariable possession of the whole of His unlimited Life, together and at once: *Vitae interminabilis, tota, simul, et perfecta possessio.*—EDWARDS.

between the Ways and Purposes of God, is specially important in its application to the determination of the Divine Mind respecting the final destinies of mankind. With very special explicitness and emphasis is the connection declared in Scripture between the agency and the purposes of God in this high matter. Equally explicit and emphatic is the verification of the Biblical word by the facts of history and experience. In the sphere of human knowledge nothing is exhibited in a more outstanding and prominent manner than this connection. Manifestly and palpably it has been the design of God to set this connection forth to the view of mankind, so as to leave no place for reasonable doubt concerning it. Among a multitude of inspired testimonies relating to this subject, see the ninth chapter of the Epistle to the Romans, and the words of our Lord in Mat. xi. 25–27. If the agency and the purpose of God, in this respect, have one and the same vindication, there is herein, as we shall see, no cause for stumbling or dissatisfaction with the latter.

Let His agency, in part, be considered. First, He makes an atonement, by the sacrifice of His Son, for the sins of all mankind; the greatest of all the wonders of His goodness. Next, through the virtue of this atonement, He introduces His Spirit into the world as the renewer and sanctifier of human nature,— the next greatest of His mercies. Then in direct connection with these mighty doings of infinite goodness, the proclamation of grace is made indiscriminately to all. Added to these, a system of suasory appliances is appointed, in which the Spirit strives with men with an urgency which forbears nothing but compulsion. Finally, after resistance on the part of all, not to be overcome by all these amazing measures of Divine love, a discrimination appears; the inward work of the Spirit is wrought in some, and not wrought in others; the former receive the atonement, and are saved; the others continue to reject it, and perish.

Such are the Ways of God in their order. Excepting the final one, unquestionably they demand adoring praise and wonder; and as to the exception, the discrimination of sovereignty, what but blasphemy can ask, "What doest Thou?" Either God must perform the inward work of His Spirit in whom He will perform it, or perform it in all, or consign all to destruction. Excluding the last, the choice lies between the other two. The demand that He do the second were impious; for who knows that He would not, by doing it, dishonor Himself, and so destroy the happiness of the universe? The first, therefore, remains as the only alternative: God must exercise His prerogative of showing mercy, in this form, to whom it seems best to Himself to show it.

In doing this, it is denying His Deity to suppose that He acts without a sufficient reason. What the reason is we know not, and doubtless can never fully know; nor have we a right to demand the reason; nor is it certain that the knowledge of it would be for our advantage. But in ignorance of the reason, we know enough to command our praise. The objects of the Divine preference, it is true, are not always those human wisdom would have selected. There are not many mighty, or noble, or wise ones of the world among them. But three facts are certain to us: First, not one of the human race can claim to be preferred for the sake of anything in or done by himself, or on the ground of compliance with conditions, there being no such compliance before the choice goes into effect. Secondly, the Divine agency generally exerts itself, not in the absence of proper activities, whether on the part of the chosen, or of others on their behalf, but on the contrary, in the midst of such activities, and so as to encourage and stimulate them in the highest degree. And thirdly, the perfection of the Divine Character makes it certain that there is nothing which should have influence on the determination of the mind of God, which has not this influence on it in its precise measure and weight. Such is the Divine agency in reference to the heirs of salvation.

In respect to the others, there is one essential point of difference as to the reason of the Divine determination. We have important knowledge as to this reason; it lies in something within themselves. The elect are not elected because of any goodness of their own. It is for the sake of sin, wilful, persistent, incorrigible sin in themselves, that the others are reprobated. God waits to be gracious to them, until to wait longer is forbidden by goodness itself. They fill up the measure of their iniquity; justice performs its strange work upon them; they are abandoned to their own wilfulness; they are judicially hardened, and sealed to the day of perdition. Such is the Divine conduct; it is its own vindication. According to what has been demonstrated, there is no difference as to vindication between this conduct and the eternal purpose which it fullfils.

Aversion is often expressed, and doubtless, oftener felt, towards the doctrine of God's purposes. But nothing is more unreasonable than this aversion, nothing of higher importance than the doctrine which provokes it. The world needs to know that there is no chance, no place for chance, in the dominions of its Almighty Maker and Sovereign. That all things are moving forward under the direction of an intelligence, a will, and a goodness which secures their infallible convergence and consummation in their appointed end, is no less certain than that God exists, and no less necessary than this, as a foundation for human hope and peace.

10

III.—MYSTERY.

In the idea of God, the world, comprising an immense variety of parts, is an absolute unit or whole. As a whole, it is what it is from the relation and unition of its parts, one with another; and each of its parts is what it is from its membership with the whole; all its antecedents, concomitants and sequents, and their interdependence on one another, contribute to give it its individuality. I am what I am, and everything in me, and pertaining to me, is what it is, from an exigency in the organism of the Universe, which acts upon me, and upon which, in some measure, I reciprocally act; whence it follows that it is impossible to comprehend any, the least part of the world, without ability to comprehend the entire world. I can no more understand why I am what I am, or why my bodily configuration, or size, or temperament, or any part of me, is distinctively what it is, than why the sum of existence, comprising the various worlds and creatures which make it up, is the aggregate of these, instead of others in their place.

And as with the creation, so likewise with Providence, the management of the creation; ability to comprehend the whole, is the indispensable condition of comprehending any part. The plan of Providence is also a unit. The purposes of the Infinite Mind, though they do not begin and end like ours, exist in an order in which they are related, one to all the others, and these to that, at the demand of absolute unity or system. The purpose which now goes into effect has fitting respect to every other Divine purpose, and is what it is, from its being an integrant in a system of purposes, or in one comprehensive and all-controlling purpose. The dispensations of Providence, and all particular acts and arrangements under them, imply one another; so that the indispensable prerequisite of comprehending anything whatever in the course of Providence is a complete knowledge of everything included in the entire scheme of Providence.

And if God's works be mysterious to us, how much more His Nature! A Being who exists, not by will, but of necessity; whose non-existence is an impossibility even to omnipotence; in whom nothing begins or ends; the very idea of whom excludes time, with all its successions and changes; to whom nothing is new or old; absolutely free, yet whose choices and affections are eternally immanent and the same—how far must such a Being transcend forever the utmost reach of finite thought! There are, it is true, certain predications which we may make concerning Him, assuming that certain perfections belong to Him, with which we are acquainted. If He is wise, and just, and good, since we know the qualities which these terms express, we know that He is incapable of everything self-evidently the opposite of them; nay, more, we know that He cannot but prefer a greater to a less good; he cannot disown the principle of Optimism. But beyond such inevitable intuitions, we can, of ourselves, neither affirm nor deny anything as to the contents, or capabilities, or requisitions of His infinite Nature. Not even through a revelation from Himself, however perfect, can we ever know more than a part of what He is, and a part less than nothing, compared to what remains.

To creatures, therefore, mystery in the ways of God is and ever will be a necessity. What the greatest good required, what world, what order of creatures, what disposition of them, what revelations of Himself and of Truth, what plans and acts of Providence were necessary to the realization of this good, only God Himself could know. If an intelligence, large as He could have created, be supposed to have existed when He was about to begin His works, it could have had no anticipation of the first or any other one of these; or have conjectured any single step of an agency which was to move under the direction of perfect foreknowledge of all the possibilities, contingencies and futuritions embraced in the scheme of operations from beginning to end. How utterly ignorant must it have been, as to what should be the limit of the Creation, or whether in time it should have a limit; or, whether such orders of creatures as the angelic and human should be brought into being—or if so, how related to each other; whether there should have been such a pre-Adamite earth as that which preceded the creation of man; or, what constitution of things man should be put under; or, in the event of his fall, what thereafter behooved to be done through the progress of time, until the final consummation! How forcible on this point the questions put to Job, by the Almighty Himself, out of the whirlwind!

Nor is it in any respect to our disadvantage, or, so far as we can see, inconsistent with Optimism, that the ways of God should be a mystery to us. On the contrary, mystery is itself one of the means of the greatest good—an indispensable means. That God should be evermore, both in Himself and as to the full significance of His works—DEUS ABSCONDITUS—a God who hideth Himself from us, is essential to our highest good. It is to His own glory, and therefore to our advantage, that He remain for ever unsearchable and past finding out to perfection. He were no longer a God to us if He were not to our apprehension the Incomprehensible; the infinite would be no more. It is not the part of true science, it is the renunciation alike of reason and of piety, to stumble at mystery. The highest illumination, the profoundest philosophy, the greatest virtue and happiness of a creature is attained, when, with an adoring sense of the unfathomable Being and counsels of God, he can utter from the lowest depths of his soul such words as these of the humble Psalmist: "Lord, my heart is not haughty, nor mine eyes lofty; neither do I exercise myself in great matters, nor in things too high for me. Surely I have behaved and quieted myself, as a child that is weaned from his mother; my soul is even as a weaned child."

IV.—HAPPINESS.

Among objects, ideal or real, some are pleasing, some only unpleasing or painful. The latter, *for their own sake*, cannot be desired or regarded as good. If they are ideal merely, goodness forbids their becoming real; if they are real, it requires their destruction. Only the possibility that good ulterior to themselves may be educed from them, can make their actuality consistent with the dominion of goodness. Objects which only give pain, apart from the possibility of their being in some way made useful, are simply noxious. There can be no such objects, in reality, under the requisition of goodness; they can exist only in idea.

If things simply and absolutely painful might be supposed to be good in themselves, their realization were not to be desired. But such things are not in themselves good. Even the sublime goodness, which suffered in the Person of Christ, would not have been goodness if it was to have had no fruit of goodness, or if its sufferings had terminated in themselves. Better would it have been, on that supposition, that they had never been a reality. They were, in truth, not good—not in any view desirable.

It is thus manifest that goodness presupposes good

in its ultimation; to be goodness, it must tend to and result in good, or have its fruit unto happiness. That is not goodness which in itself, and its uses or results, is pure and permanent unhappiness. The estate and the fruit of goodness may be unhappy for a time, through its own sacrifices for the sake of good, or the abuse it receives from its enemies; but that goodness should in no way and at no time result in happiness, or in less happiness than it foregoes or denies itself, is a contradiction; and this, in principle, proportions the value of goodness to its utility or fruitfulness in happiness. The tree of goodness, as our Lord taught, is known by its fruits; fruits of absolute unhappiness or pain for its own sake, show that the tree which produces them is not a good one; the greater the fruits of happiness, on the other hand, the more excellent the tree.

The manner of the connection of happiness with goodness, or how the latter is to result in the former, is not always obvious; as far as can be seen, there is, perhaps, no mode in which the two can be conjoined; nevertheless goodness assumes the absolute and final disconnection to be impossible: goodness trusts in itself as the principle or agent of good; has the assurance of faith where sight is denied it, as to its appropriate ultimation; anticipates the advance of happiness, as the end of its painful sacrifices, when these it is called to make. Amidst its greatest sufferings, compensatory joy is set before it; it casts its bread upon the waters, assured of receiving it again after many days, if not sooner; it does not doubt, when it goes forth and weeps, bearing precious seed, that it shall come again with rejoicing, bringing its sheaves with it: applying the most "crucial" of tests to it, it will be found to have happiness, its own or others, as its ultimate end.

The doctrine that goodness has utility or happiness for its principle and last end, cannot be reproached, without first doing an injury to happiness, by disconnecting its idea from that of goodness and setting it forth in this dishonorable isolation. The two ideas, in truth, are neither separate nor separable. As goodness must comprehend happiness, virtually, in order to be goodness, so happiness, in its chief element, is goodness itself. Not only is the good man the only happy one, but it is his goodness, more than aught else, that makes him happy. Goodness, for goodness and happiness' sake, may suffer pain; but while it thereby advances itself, it is potential happiness, in an equal degree, to its subject and others. In this view of happiness our Lord appears transcendent in it, above all others, in the extremity of His passion. In a full view of His estate, there was not, out of the sphere of the Infinite, one as happy as He was amidst the overwhelming flood of His piacular sorrows.

It is only by identifying happiness with present enjoyment, or assuming that there is no happiness, in so far as pleasurable feeling is interrupted, that Christ, in His sufferings, can be esteemed unhappy. Let happiness be taken as including goodness in itself; or, instead of naming it happiness, let it be called GOOD— its completest name; and its just and inevitable distinction is that of the GREATEST GOOD—the pursuit and goal of Optimism.

It follows from what has been said, that the only absolute unhappiness is *sin*—that is to say, rebellion against goodness. This, in its very idea, is the adversary of happiness. It must be counteracted and defeated, to prevent its proving the destruction of universal good. Everything else may be made by goodness to subserve the greatest good; sin is an exception. The sinner's only hope is in repentance and forgiveness. Incorrigible impenitence is necessary ruin.

10*

V.—SIN.

Sin, or moral evil, is absolutely or only evil. Other evils, which are made necessary by sin, are means of good ; but sin is the *means* of no good, in the strict sense of the expression. It would, on the contrary, destroy all good, if not effectually counteracted. In a system in which sin has place, other evils may not be ultimately evil, but good—things, on the whole, to be desired. They may counterwork sin, undo its mischief, prevent further mischief from it ; cultivate goodness ; subserve the pursuit of the highest good attainable after sin has entered. But sin itself, which gave occasion for these evils, would, in its destructiveness of good, hinder them also from promoting good, and work, through them, to the increase of itself ; and would pervert everything else unto evil, and so make the condition of the universe merely evil, and the nonexistence of the universe an object of desire. The ills of life, so called, the afflictions of good men, the chastisements of God, the severest punishments of sin, are, in a comprehensive view, the means of good—the necessary means of the greatest good, *where sin is to be encountered* ; hell itself is so, regarded as the punishment of sin. But sin in itself, and in its proper effects and tendencies, is simply evil, out of which good, as its natural product, can no more come than light out of darkness, sweet out of bitter, cold from burning heat. Optimism, therefore, which, in principle and activity, seeks only good, has no need of sin, and as a means adapted, in itself, to an end, can make no use of it; on the contrary, it has, from first to last, to work against it and destroy its works. It may have to take occasion from it to employ instruments and agencies of its own, which, in the absence of sin, would have been unnecessary. It may turn the machinations of sin against itself, and thus produce good, not otherwise to be attained; but this good is from its own activity, in contending against sin; not from sin as an agent or means of good. The word MEANS is sometimes used in a loose sense, in which it includes whatever forms of instrumental agency may spring incidentally from urgent occasions; as when *e.g.*, a pestilence is said to be a means of health, because it occasioned the invention of medicinal or other remedies against future visitations of the calamity. But there is, in such a use of language, no intention of confounding *means* and *occasions;* or, to take the illustration just instanced, to say that the pestilence, and the remedies bear the same relation to health. The pestilence was the means of death or disease; the means of health were the remedies, of the invention or application of which the pestilence was the occasion. Whether of the remedies or their effects, the pestilence was a means, only in the sense in which everything is said to be a means, which leads, however incidentally or casually, to results ulterior to itself.

Sin, instead of being the means of the greatest good,

is a means of preventing this, in so far as sin, with its proper effects, cannot be excluded, under the best mode of agency which can be employed for the purpose. The good attainable in the absence of sin, was greater than that which could be attained after its entrance; otherwise, sin was the indispensable condition of the greatest good, originally; and the earnest pursuit of this, while repelling, or seeking to prevent sin, was impossible, unless one may be in earnest in seeking to defeat his own ends.

But though sin be not the means of good, may not the remedy of sin, with its evils, have been originally necessary to the greatest good? If it was, then, the greatest good, demanding this remedy as indispensable to its attainment, demanded, at the same time, sin—apart from which there was no place for the remedy; and the answer to the question has already been given. It may be that advantage may come from a remedy beyond that which was directly sought from it; but to make a remedy originally necessary to the greatest advantage, is to make the evil—that is, in the present case, sin—also necessary, without which there is no need or place for the remedy. Where there is a disease, there may be nothing better than a remedy for it; but it were better, if it might be so, to have neither disease nor remedy. He surely were "a physician of no value," however famous as a curer of disease, who makes the disease which he cures.

As the plan of the world involved the possibility and the futurition of evil—though to be prevented, if it might be, under the best preventive agency—the Divine Goodness, to which all things in the world's appointed course were manifest, could not but have had reference to the rise of sin, and anticipated and provided against it even from the beginning; and the arrangement and ordering of all things in creation and providence could not but have been accordingly determined on. But this proleptical or prudential reference no more interfered with the desire of the the Deity that sin might not be, or with His using proper means to prevent it, than does his foresight of the future certainty of sin, now. God did, from the first, as He now does, oppose Himself to sin. He did not and does not want it. It is, as it ever has been and must be, the abominable thing which His soul hateth. He made all things good; it was desirable, that is to say, it was for the best, that they should remain so. He used the best agency to keep them so. It was not best to depart from this agency, in order to prevent the dire change which was made in the state of the world by sin. Better than this variation from His established order, was inflexible adherence to it, together with the Remedial Scheme which He purposed to introduce, upon the perpetration of sin. But it was not better for the change to take place. Sin gave occasion for new procedures of Divine goodness, which was still intent on gaining the greatest good now achievable; but that this was greater than that which would have been attainable, if sin had not entered, supposes either that God preferred a less good to a greater, as the end of His works, or that

He had need of sin, the enemy of all good and the cause of evil, of which He only can know the magnitude, in order to gain the greater; each of which would undeify Him. It does not hence follow that there was a change or an after-thought in the mind of God. The only thing necessary to be assumed is, that God, the Infinite and Incomprehensible, is incapable of any agency inconsistent with goodness, or with sincerity in opposing or resisting sin. An assumption contravening the theory of the universe, which makes Redemption or the Remedial system the prime end of the Divine agency in creation and providence. All things were made by and for Him, who, in due time, became the Redeemer of man; but—except in the system of the Divine purposes, of which the order is anti-typical to that of events—He was not a Redeemer when they were made; and the prolepsis, or anticipation of Redemption, was not inconsistent with the earnest use of the best agency for preventing the necessity for it.

VI.—THE REIGN OF SIN.

Volition, the act of willing, follows prevailing desire, or what appears best at the moment of its occurrence; and under the influence of sin, this appearance always belongs to evil. It is the peculiar function of sin, to make evil seem the greatest good, when an exercise of the will is about to put itself forth, under its command. It is impossible that evil, as such, or for its own sake, should be preferred before good; it is also impossible, that to the view of any one, however debased by sin, evil and good, as such, should exchange qualities or lose their essential distinctiveness from one another. Nevertheless, while, and in so far as sin reigns within any one, his preference is steadfast and inevitable in favor of evil. It is the work of sin to produce this preference; that is, as before said, to make evil appear more desirable than good—or better, at the moment of volition, than any good in its stead. Here, at a glance, is seen the nature of the Dominion of Sin. Its beginning is in Deceit; the sinner is drawn away of his own desire, and enticed; hence a false appearance, wherein is the inception, and the elemental life or essence of sin. (See James i. 14, 15, and compare Genesis iii. 6.) Thus it is that sin, the enemy of good, whose good is evil, begins its work of death. It does its first mischief in deluding the sinner; it is to him a voluntary enslavement to delusion; it makes him the victim of false appearance; it starts him in a career of desperate enmity to good and goodness in himself; and according to this mad beginning, he pursues his way, the agent of his own ruin, and fitted to be an instrument of ruin in the world.

The history of sin, presents it as an organized Empire. The first sinner was an angel. We know nothing as to the manner of his fall; whether it originated in a confederacy with others, or whether they became his confederates after its occurrence, we are not informed; but he appears in the history of our world, under the name of SATAN, as the supreme head of an empire, and as such holds a place of impious rivalry and defiance to the Almighty Maker and Ruler Himself. Already "the prince" of evil angels, he sought to add the race of man to the number of his subjects, and the record of his success stands in the foreground of the sad fortunes of mankind. Thenceforth, he became "the prince," or "god," as he is variously called, of this world also; a bad eminence, which he has always found it too easy to maintain. The earth, consequently, is the seat of a kingdom of Satan, having its own compact, its own constitution and laws, its own most effective administration, and the nations and generations of men in voluntary subjection to it. Through this mighty organism, sin is ever and everywhere working to the destruction of good, and the multiplication of evil, with a force and to an extent not to be computed.

The accomplishment of the arch-adversary's design

against man, required but one attempt. The race existing in germ, in a common sire, from whom it was to spring in successive generations, fell in his fall—the natural result of the debasement of humanity in him. Success with Adam was the success with his posterity. The race was lost in him. Until man shall cease to be born of woman, flesh to be born of flesh, each individual, when he comes into the world, will be "by nature a child of wrath, shapen in iniquity and conceived in sin." The contrary could not be, but by superseding natural by the intervention, in every instance, of supernatural force ; which, if the principle of Optimism determined the first arrangement, could not be admitted—the consequence to be excluded by it, being, in the Divine view, in that case, not so undesirable as the intervention itself would be on the whole. The result, therefore, was inevitable. Through a perversion of the constitution under which our nature had its beginning, the first man's ruin was the ruin of mankind.

Nor has the perversion of Divine order in the interest of sin been restricted to this fundamental instance. Man was to live in families, in communities, in cities, in states ; in each of these were to be spheres of closer affinity, fellowships of pleasure, of trade, of science, and letters, etc.; whence special customs, modes of life, maxims, principles of action, compacts, etc., each forming a distinct centre of influence. All have been perverted, and all, through perversion, have contributed to enlarge immeasurably the predominance of sin. And the more so, immeasurably, because on the whole, and in each particular, the original enemy, with the evil principalities and powers under his command, has never ceased to apply the machinations of his own industrious sagacity. Nor is the view of perversion yet complete. It has been extended through the entire physical sphere, all natural agencies and forces—the light, the air, all the elements, all the ordinances of heaven and earth: to use sacred language, " the whole creation," subsidized by sin, " has been made to groan and travail together in pain until now."

Moreover, sin has its own individual organisms—establishments directly formed by itself; fellowships and foundations originally intended and constructed as engines of evil; institutions of error, idolatry, iniquity of every form, vast and manifold, in and through which the various agents of evil operate, with every advantage for success, all under the control and energy of the prime Author of evil.

The actual varieties in which sin has appeared in human life, and its triumphant progress from age to age, correspond with these great facilities for extending and demonstrating its power. Its expression toward man himself has been in every form of lust, deception, injustice, rapine, murder, cruelty, violence; toward God, in irreverence, insult, blasphemy, idolatry, atheism; in which, and in all their subordinate forms, it has, in all time, overspread the face of the earth, as the waters cover the sea. Before the flood, every imagination of the thoughts of man's heart being only evil continually, all flesh corrupted its way on the earth, and filled it with violence; insomuch that, in the language of the sacred record, it repented God and grieved Him at His heart that He had made man. From its second beginning until the advent of Christ, the course of mankind is traced in the first chapter of the Epistle to the Romans; with which profane records fully concur; and this transcript of atrocity is equally applicable to the generations which have followed.

And it immensely enhances the evil of sin's enormities among men, that it has put them all forth, against incessant opposition to it, on the part of the Divine goodness. For, after the first transgression of man, the Remedial scheme, the best which that goodness could devise, immediately began to exert itself. Atonement was anticipated, punishment was stayed, pardon was offered to repentance, institutions of grace were appointed, and in every appropriate mode, the agency of the Holy Spirit was exerted. Nor was it only in forms of forbearance and gentleness, that the goodness of God strove against sin. It employed severity as well as pity; it arrayed against incorrigible impenitence the terrors of Avenging justice; it set forth signal examples of this justice, to induce others to repent; through judicial abandonments it exhibited sin as dreadfully punishing itself, by the multiplication of monstrous forms of evil; it pointed man to whole nations, one after another, one by means of others, perishing through their sinfulness; it announced eternal death and hell as following on the heels of obstinate guilt; in fearful sights and signs, in shakings and convulsions of nature, it sounded loud alarms to the world.

Thus God has contended, and thus He is still contending against sin, which appears in the greatness and terribleness of its dominion, in that even against such opposition to it, it can not only maintain itself, but pervert this very opposition into the occasion of its self-aggrandisement. How eminent among mysteries, this most outstanding fact of the mutual militancy of sin and the Divine goodness! Yet even above this, as cause for amazement, stands another very familiar fact—namely, that men, with knowledge of the former fact, and with bitter experience in themselves of the deadliness of the reign of sin, and often with lively apprehensions of the peril of final and absolute subjugation to it, in the eternity to come, impending over them every moment, still, by their own choice, keep themselves exposed to this peril.

VII.—MERCY.

There is in sentient being, so far as we are acquainted with it, a self-protective property called *anger*, which, on a sudden attack, instantly springs into exercise against the assailant. But in rational creatures this constitutional element is under the law of goodness, against the interest of which its indulgence is not to be allowed. When, therefore, its proper end, self-protection, ceases to require its exercise, it should be suppressed, since it would produce only pain or unhappiness, which, if not necessary, is inconsistent with the rule of goodness. A good being cannot indulge anger for no purpose: simply vindictive or malign anger resteth nowhere, except in the bosom of fools. (Eccles. vii. 9.)

If this property belong to the nature of the Deity, it must in Him, also, be subordinate to goodness, the glory of every good being. The All-Perfect, the pattern of perfection to His creatures, can give no expression to useless anger. The Scripture ascribes this feeling to the Divine Being, in the strongest terms of irascible passion: "God is jealous, and the Lord revengeth; the Lord revengeth and is furious; the Lord will take vengeance on His adversaries, and He reserveth wrath for His enemies." (Nah. i. 2.) But to apply such language to God, in a sense supposing Him to be revengeful, like a man infuriated with malignant passion, were to set the Scripture into discord with itself, and to make the Deity an object of infinite horror to His creatures. Over every thing in the constitution and essence, and entire agency of God, the supremacy of goodness is immanent and absolute. His anger, in its highest manifestations, its severest inflictions, is the servitor and agent of His goodness. If it destroys some, it is because something worse would be involved in sparing them. If it makes a hell, it does this work of indignant justice, because in not doing it, it would cease to be goodness, or refrain from using the necessary means of the greatest good. It has had to do this dreadful work. The first sinners, the devil and his angels, are reserved under chains of everlasting darkness; and the same is the inevitable doom of those of mankind who will not forsake their fellowship. For the way of goodness is not that of mere will: it has its own indispensable and immutable conditions. It would defeat itself, it would, in effect, cease to be goodness, if it did not observe proper mode; or if it disregarded moral proportion or harmony in its actings. God cannot act out of harmony with Himself. He were no longer God, if, in any movement, in or out of Himself, there were a non-concurrence of any one of His perfections; if, *e.g.*, He should put forth an exercise of *power* from which *wisdom* should dissent; or an exercise of *mercy* against the protest of *justice*. In strictest truth, what God, as GOD, can do, is not what power or mercy can do—for God is more than power or mercy—but what can be done by an activity in which every divine attribute can combine and coalesce. It is one of the worst fruits of sin, that an opinion which denies this highest of necessities prevails among men. They think the goodness of God may take the form of mercy by arbitrary will; on this assumption they reason and construct their theories and systems;—an assumption which is itself virtually the sum of delusion, involving the undeifying of God, the end of all good and goodness in the universe.

There was, as the event proved, a possibility of showing mercy to man, when he brought the need of it on himself. But this possibility had its ground in another, namely, the possibility to the Divine goodness, of so preparing its way to take the form of *mercy*, that it might do so and yet remain goodness to the end; or not do ultimately more evil than good. There was this latter possibility, but the ground of it did not lie in simple will or power, but in a sufficiency and a readiness in the Divine goodness to make a self-sacrifice, which was itself the highest instance of that goodness, and the comprehension of all the good thenceforth to be communicated to mankind. Two subordinate ends required to be answered: First, the adequate revelation of Avenging justice, or the Divine displeasure against sin, the measure of which is nothing less than that of the Divine goodness itself, since of this goodness and all its possible fruits, sin is the enemy and would be the destroyer; and, secondly, the application of an agency by which sin itself can be destroyed, and the original order restored in those to whom the sacrifice is ultimately available; since, otherwise, the effect of the sacrifice would be but to promote and aggrandize the power of sin. Self-evidently these two were indispensable prerequisites to the course of goodness toward man. And incidental to them, there was this contingence, namely, the aggravation of final unhappiness to such as might, in persistent contempt of goodness, choose to abide under the dominion of sin. The conditions involving the contingency were met: the possibility became a reality. THE REIGN OF MERCY was instituted: Goodness—establishing itself on its own firm and everlasting foundation; meeting all exigencies of Holy justice; securing itself against ultimate defeat and abuse—changed its original form, and, thenceforth, instead of simple kindness or favor, became favor to THE GUILTY; wherein, in countless varieties, and in fulness, as that of the sea, it has abounded to mankind.

It is impossible to us to know in what respects goodness had to forego its first course of agency, the course it would have pursued, if sin had been unknown. A different object was now before it. Known unto God are all His works from the beginning of the world; the end ultimately to be attained by them must, therefore, have also been known to Him; but this, before the entrance of sin, did not hinder His earnestly pursuing the end which might have been attained in the absence of sin; else, as has been already said, God's foreknowledge would subject Him altogether to Fate,—that is to say, there were in truth no God. And if He did aim at this end, means suited to its attainment must have been employed by Him. What they were, or, beyond the negative intuitions of reason, what they were not, it were presumptuous in us to attempt to imagine, much more to claim, as too many have done, to have positive knowledge. Not contingent possibilities or requisitions, but inspired teaching and the facts of history and experience, are what we are concerned with. According to these, the economy of goodness proceeding on its new basis, was wonderfully new in many fundamental particulars. It required Human Nature to be constituted anew, under a new Head, and in a new Root. It made new conditions and terms of favor with God; it appointed new institutions and ordinances of life; it gave access to new resources of strength and happiness; it opened new prospects; it made new promises, and threatened new penalties; it called for a new and highly peculiar form of character; it involved new and stupendous fortunes to mankind.

It applied its provisions and influences to the entire race; it blessed the entire race with mercies innumerable, and of immeasurable value. But it did not at once undo the perversions and mischiefs of sin; it did not restore at once the original order of the world; it did not abolish natural evils; it did not exclude temptation or the tempter; it did not reverse the sentence of bodily dissolution, or exempt man from disappointment, pain, or any form of disease; it did not preclude enmities among men toward one another; it left itself subject to malignant opposition from evil angels and men; it was to make its way through desperate conflicts, and alternate success and defeat, to be continued to the end of time ; and at last the dire necessity would remain to it of consigning the impenitent to enhanced unhappiness.

The manifestations and achievements of Goodness, both before and after the change of its way, will at last demonstrate the undeviating supremacy of Optimism in the universe. It will then be made evident that as the best world was brought into existence by creative power, so the best management of it will have been maintained through the entire course of time. There will be nothing to be excepted, nothing instead of which something better might have been done. Not so good would have been the agency necessary to prevent the entrance of sin, as that negative agency which permitted this, connected with its sequel, the institution of the Reign of mercy. Not better would it have been to have employed a different agency to that which was exerted to prevent the predominance of sin and the doom of the lost. Still it will remain self-evident that greater good would have been possible if sin, with its evils, had never been known. The doing of mercy will fill Heaven with eternal wonder and joy ; it will make revelations of goodness which but for it would have had no place ; God, in one aspect of His character, will be known, as otherwise He could not have been. But better, nevertheless, had it been if no occasion for the exercise of His mercy had arisen ; if His goodness had been left to pursue its course as goodness simply ; to employ its unsearchable resources for the production of goodness and happiness in the universe, without a necessity for a Hell. The inflictions of Avenging justice in punishing incorrigible sin, are not to be spared; they produce a sense, as salutary as it is awful, of the majesty of law, and the strength and stability of government. But it is pure malignity only that can refrain from regret at the demand for them; and it is only this demand, this inexorable necessity, that enables goodness to reconcile itself to them.

VIII.—THE REDEEMER.

AMONG things of highest certainty to us, are those to which our ideas of *personality* and *essence* correspond, and the radical difference between these two. And though we cannot define or explain them, the knowledge of them and of their difference from each other cannot but be assumed in common intellection and discourse; nor can there be any justness of continuous thinking or expression on subjects of greatest moment, without carefully distinguishing between them, so that nothing shall ever be predicated of one which is peculiar to the other.

Of finite persons, so far as we know, each one has a distinct and a single personality proper to himself; but personality in them may, in the same individual, be united to several essences or natures. Thus, the same man with one personality, is a compound of body and spirit, the essences of which are not only diverse, but immiscible. Of the Deity, whose essence is infinite, the opposite of this has been revealed to us. He has but one Essence, but this dwells completely in three distinct Persons, from eternity and of necessity united, and so constituting one God.

By that wisdom of the world, which with God is foolishness, the Tri-personality of the Supreme Being is rejected; using, in doing so, its own absolute ignorance to deprive itself of knowledge of highest concernment, and thus giving a pre-eminent example of the Deceit and infatuation in which sin had its beginning, and by which it has strengthened and extended its dominion.

In rejecting this sublime revelation, a sinful world virtually abolishes all hope for itself. It was the peculiarity as to the mode or constitution of the Divine Being, which this revelation announces, that enabled infinite Goodness, so to speak, to continue its course toward fallen man in the form of MERCY. Herein lay the ground of the possibility of its making the prerequisite sacrifice. It was impossible for us to have known of ourselves what this sacrifice behooved to be; but as it required to have a value satisfactory to Avenging Justice, or equivalent to that of the punishment of sin, according to its demerit, it is self-demonstrative that it could be made by no finite or created person. In the sphere of the finite there is no person competent to make, or undertake to make it. However exalted or endowed, however eminent in rank or goodness, finite persons may be, they depend on the Infinite for whatever they are and have; and to deny or lose a sense of this dependence, would be to become atheistic, or make themselves gods. There is absurdity, not to say impiety, in the idea that such persons, unless already fallen into the delusiveness of sin, should think themselves capable of more goodness than is already due from them to their Maker on their own account. How, then, shall they be able, or think themselves able, to make satisfaction for sin, or the want of goodness in another; much less in a whole race of creatures? If, therefore, the sacrifice was required to be made by a Person, he must be a Divine one; that is to say, a Person in the sphere, and having the essence of the Infinite; and if there had been but one such Person, he must have been that one; a necessity, as we shall see, involving another necessity, namely, that for a time there should be no Divine Person in the estate of glory proper to the Divine Being; the idea of which is no less absurd and monstrous than that of blank atheism.

Which of the Divine Persons should assume the undertaking was of necessity determinable only by themselves. There was one of them called by various names,—the Word, the Life, the only begotten Son of God,—by whom, in a special sense, though with concurrence of the others, all acts and operations of the Deity in the world and in its creation had been performed. On Him this work also was devolved, and by Him it was accomplished.

Its accomplishment required of Him an infinite humiliation. He had to descend into the sphere of humanity, and to take humanity completely, its sinfulness alone excepted, into a personal union with His Divine Nature. His eternal Personality, divesting itself of the form proper to Him as Divine, was to appear thenceforth, for a human lifetime, in fashion as that of a man; in which, by additional abasement, in all respects extreme, He had to finish His undertaking. In this descent from the rank of the Infinite, He could not cease Himself to be Infinite: God cannot undeify

Himself. Accordingly, in the descent, even down to its lowest depth, the honors due only to the Deity were still paid to Him; as in its sequel, He showed Himself still Divine by Divine works of His own, and was also witnessed unto and sealed, as having coequal Divinity with themselves by the other Divine Persons. Nevertheless, except that He knew no sin, the measure of His humiliation was throughout without measure; and, at its last stage especially, it was unsearchably strange and wonderful. In its process to this stage, He presents an example of wisdom in teaching, of self-denying beneficence, of patient endurance of temptation and affliction, of meekness and self-composure under the greatest provocations, wherein His Divine-Human character is also resplendent with brightest glory to those who are competent to discern it. But now, a tragical scene occurs, which stands alone even in this wondrous history of God-man abasement. As to its direct causes, it is to us absolutely incomprehensible; yet one fact sufficiently explains it. Having made Himself answerable to Eternal Justice for the sins of mankind; their sins, in the language of Scripture, were laid upon Him, to be avenged in His sacred person; nor was He spared any, the least portion, of the infliction required of Him by that terrible justice. This infliction was not the same,—it could not have been the same,—which it would have been if it had been received by us in our persons; but it was what only He, as uniting in Himself the finite with the infinite, could have either sustained or received. It dealt with "Him who knew no sin," as if, to use inspired language, He had been "Sin itself," the embodiment of whatever could be called sin. It expressed itself in effects and demonstrations answerable to this representation. Not only in insult, mockery, scourging, crucifixion, from those for whom he suffered, but in prayers and supplications, with strong crying and tears, to Him who was able to save Him from death; in a sweat, as it were, of great drops of blood, falling down to the ground; in a loud outcry on the cross, in which He proclaimed Himself forsaken of God; and, finally, in a preternatural death, succeeded by entombment in "the heart of the earth." These, attended by profoundly symbolical phenomena of nature, in heaven and earth, and the shades of death, are the interpreters to the world of what has been called emphatically THE PASSION of the Redeemer. They do not explain its psychology, or mode of possibility, or how the finite and infinite could have the interagency which was involved in it; but the knowledge of this, which doubtless no finite mind is capable of receiving, was not necessary. The facts which God has made as ever living, ever present realities in the eyes of the world, are sufficient. It is enough that these facts, by the ordering of God, set forth, like the sun in the firmament, the great certainty they involve, namely, that one of the Divine Trinity, leaving His estate of glory with his coequals in Godhead, and assuming under His Divine Personality the nature of man, became the subject of such humiliation and suffering as the facts attest—this was enough. The demonstration could not be made greater that the satisfaction to Justice was complete, the indignation of the Divine goodness against sin adequately revealed.

There remains, however, another consideration which immensely increases the estimation of this doing of Divine Love. It is that of the Relationship of the God-man to the other Divine Persons. The eternally Three-one are in their unity eternally *related* to each other. They are so of necessity, even as they are of necessity united in the essence. And their inter-relations are grounds of special affections and interagencies among them. As a fact,—a fact unexplained and doubtless unexplainable,—God has affirmed nothing concerning His Deity, not even His essential unity, more explicit than this. Especially, He has announced nothing more impressively, than that He who bore the sins of mankind was a Person of ineffable nearness and endearment to Himself. He calls Him His own, His only begotten Son. And, farther, He tells us, that this His Son, who offered Himself as a sacrifice for us, was His own *gift* to us. The essential coequality of this Person with the other Divine Persons, made it impossible that He should be given against His own desire; but that desire presupposed, His Filial relationship to God, gave possibility to His being given of His Eternal Father, and the possibility became real. So that a complete statement of the subject requires the assertion, that in order that Mercy, in the fulness of its blessings, might be extended to mankind, God gave His own coequal Son, who Himself desired to be so given, that through a substitutionary sacrifice made by this Divine Person, the reign of Mercy might

11*

be consistent with Justice, or be in harmony with all he Divine perfections.

This is the Atonement—anticipated from the beginning, available as soon as man fell, accomplished in due time,—it lays a foundation for the throne and dominion of Mercy firmer and more enduring than the foundation of the heavens and the earth.

IX.—THE WORK OF THE SPIRIT.

Though man, by his first disobedience, subjected himself to the despotism of sin, he did not cease to be a free agent. He was free in that act of willing, and he continued no less free afterwards. His will remained to him, with all the constitutional properties requisite to volition. He could not but will in accordance with his desire, but he was under no compulsion. There is no higher freedom—higher cannot be conceived—than that which he had: the power of willing, and opportunity to exercise it according to prevailing desire. It is, in itself, impossible to will without desire, or under no influence from former acts of willing; or, after once acting, under no disposition to one act rather than another: And if so acting was the indispensable condition of freedom, there would be no freedom in the universe; the Infinite Himself were not free, a predisposition to good volition being a necessity of His Nature.

Nevertheless, since by the immutable law of volition, the act of willing must follow desire, or the will be as the greatest apparent good, at the moment of its determination; and since evil, at that moment, always has the appearance of good, if sin has command, the certainty remains absolute of man's willing in the service of sin, until its power to deceive be overcome.

Evil will ever seem best to him, when the act of willing is to have place. The greatest good will have the appearance of evil. Urgency of persuasion, objective appliance of whatever kind, can make no difference; none, at least, in favor of the choice of good. Therefore Goodness, in order to become mercy to man, had more to do than to reveal the Divine indignation against sin, or make an atonement for it, as explained in the preceding number. It had to meet the further necessity of displacing the power of sin in man. It had to put out of its way a deep-rooted, subjective hindrance in the nature of man, as well as an objective one interposed by the Avenging justice of God, or by its own necessity of being consistent with itself, or of not so doing good, as to do evil on the whole, or fail of the greatest ultimate good. This necessity was upon it. How was it to be met? In ignorance of the condecencies, which, in truth, are necessities of the Divine activity, simple omnipotence or arbitrary will might have seemed sufficient for the purpose; but, in fact, it was not. God, as God, the All and Ever Perfect, could not so meet it. There was a possibility of meeting it, but the ground of this possibility, like that of forbearing to punish sin, lay not in the simple will or power, but in the Constitution of the Deity, as a Pluri-personal Being. This great peculiarity in the nature or constitution of the Godhead, ever an "offence" to the proud wisdom of the world, contains, in this respect also, the only foundation of hope for man. According to God's revelation of Himself to us in His Word, the economy, if we may so speak, of the agencies of the Godhead, the order of operations among the distinct Persons of the Trinity, an order depending on that of their subsistence,—ascribes the beginning of all Divine works to the First Person; their immediate production, subsistence, and sustentation, to the Second; and all concluding, completing, and perfecting acts, to the Third. With reference to the heavens and the earth (Gen. i. 2, Job xxvi. 13); to man, after his creation (Gen. ii. 7, Job xxxiii. 4); to the furnishing of man with extraordinary virtues and gifts for special works, including even the God Man Himself (Judges iii. 10, Zach. iv. 6, Is. lxi. 1), the agency in this last sphere, belongs specifically to the Spirit. It is not for us to know the reason, the fact is enough,— a fact having its basis in the Nature of the Deity, and so equalizing the necessity for the agency of the Spirit in order to displace the power of sin in man, with that of the Divine existence itself.

As it was the work of the Second Divine Person, then, to make the Atonement, so this other work without which the Atonement would have been made in vain, was the province of the Third. The two works were correlated to each other; the last depending on the first, as its indispensable condition. It was performed in the world, as was every work of Mercy, before the Atonement was actually made; but as it was needful (John xvi. 7) that the Atonement should be made before the Spirit could come in the fulness of His peculiar power, so was it, by virtue of the Atonement, anticipated, that He previously exercised His distinctive office. (Rev. xiii. 8.)

His operation, in accomplishing it, is generally two-fold, objective and subjective, outward and inward; and these, though not invariably connected, are so related to each other, that the latter seldom, if ever, has place, in adult age, if the other is wanting. The relation is not that of cause and effect, nor does it in the least interfere with the sovereignty of the Spirit in the inward operation; but the antecedence of the outward is, ordinarily, at least, indispensable to the performance of the other. With reference to the displacement of the power of sin by the inward operation, its chief end is to give a just impression of the character of that power, the fact of its all-ruinous delusiveness, its dire malignity, its utter renouncement of reason, of a pure conscience, of true self-interest, of self-respect, of the just exercise of every sentiment of humanity, as well as of the Supreme authority of infinite rectitude and goodness. It seeks to rouse up every part of man's rational, moral, godlike nature,—to make everything great and noble in man, insurgent and rebellious, against the deep debasement under which sin is holding him as its willing, most wretched captive. There is nothing, except sin itself, to which it does not direct its appeals, with the certainty, in so far as they are heeded, of a favorable response. There is in these appeals a didactic, argumentative, benign, suasory force, —that of the inspired Word of God, quick, powerful, sharper than a two-edged sword, a searcher of the thoughts and intents of the heart,—not to be resisted by anything simply human in man. And while they cannot prevail with reference to the main purpose,—

deliverance from the tyranny of sin, the effect, exclusively, of the Spirit's inward agency,—they can, in a sense, approximate this; they can make the yoke of sin too grievous to be borne; they can give a keen, intense conviction of the cruelty, the enormous wrong and iniquity, the turpitude and hatefulness of its bondage; of absolute helplessness also, or the abolition of all hope of self-deliverance; they can elicit longing, sighing, imploring outcries for aid; and so, peradventure, make it proper and suitable for the Spirit to do, what otherwise it might not seem meet, and therefore not possible for Him to do,—penetrate, with His inworking energy, to the innermost recess of nature, where sin hath its seat, and supersede its dominion by His own,—the Supreme ascendency of Truth and Holiness, over desire and consequent determinations of the will.

X.—MEDIATION.

The Atonement and the Work of the Spirit did not comprehend the whole of the Plan of Mercy to man; these were connected with another Provision of highest peculiarity.

It was not possible that the Divine Person, who was made flesh and died for our sins, should have remained under the power of death. (Acts ii. 24.) But if it had been possible it could not have proved a reality, without losing the end of His incarnation and death. The Atonement would have been completed, but it would have been without fruit. If we are reconciled to God by the *death* of His Son, it is by His *life* that we are saved. (Rom. v. 10.) Moreover, the Spirit could not have been given if Jesus had not been glorified. (John vii. 39; xiv. 7.) But immensely more was necessary—a vast sequel of administrative agency over whatsoever was to come to pass in the history of the world. The Royal authority over the universe must be committed to Christ, and exercised by Him until the end of all things. (Phil. ii. 9, 10; 1 Cor. xv. 24.)

Even before His death He had Lordship over all things. Life, death, demons, angels, the wind and seas, nature in all its spheres, took orders from Him. Nay, the Lord Jehovah, the Ruling God under the

Old Testament, was the God-man of the New Testament. But it was not until He had risen from the dead and ascended to the Father, that His solemn enthronement over the universe took place. That event was reserved as the Testimonial of God's estimation of His infinite self-abasement for man's sake. (Compare Phil. ii. 6–11 with Psalms xxiv. 7-10.) It had its reason, its ground of possibility in that self-abasement: He could not otherwise have been exalted. As a Divine Person, simply, the supremacy over all things was His already. It was originally and necessarily His; He could not have divested Himself of it. But after uniting in Himself the Human Nature to the Divine, and exchanging the Form of God for the form of a servant. He became, in this *Theanthropic*, Divine-Human character, capable of exaltation ; and God, at the proper time, made Him supreme Monarch of the whole creation, He gave Him this infinite dominion, to the end that the object of His death might be secured. (Eph. i. 22.) It was necessary that He should have it; it comprehends the potentiality, the possibility, of the full accomplishment of this object. (Eph. iv. 10.) In the fact itself of His receiving it, in the evidence hereby afforded of the infinite value of the Atonement, there was a potential bearing on the attainment of this object; but His having it was beyond this influential, and even necessary, in manifold respects. It was needed to perpetuate the virtue of the Atonement. There were, it is true, provisions on earth for this purpose ; but there was a necessity for this Heavenly provision also ; without it all earthly arrangements would have been of no avail. A vitalizing, energizing power was demanded to keep these arrangements from becoming unfruitful, perhaps even forgotten and lost; and it was only the Theanthropic kingdom that could supply this power. (Eph. i. 20–23.) But there was a necessity for Divine influences beyond the virtue of the Atonement, however perfectly conserved and actualized. The specific end of the Atonement was to remove the obstacle which our sin, as incurring the displeasure of God, had put in the way of mercy. (Romans iv. 25.) A further influence was required to fulfil the designs of mercy; one, namely, from the Resurrection of Christ. (Rom. iv. 25, second clause.) And more than even this was necessary: for neither the death of Christ nor His resurrection from the dead, by virtue of which we are *justified*, sufficed to complete our salvation. After justification we are still compassed by infirmity, and exposed to temptation and to all the forms of earthly affliction and sorrow, and are incessantly falling into new sin, so that if no further provision had been made for us the former ones would have failed. The additional exigencies were met, but they were not otherwise to be met than by the Theanthropic elevation of Christ. For the way of mercy now, as in its former stages, might not be arbitrary; the requisite aid could not come to us, from simple Will, though clothed with Omnipotence. The ability to aid us as we need had its ground in the qualifications and offices which belong to the God-man, as such, in His exalted estate. To his possession of these it was necessary that He should have had a personal experience of our trials, in the days of His flesh; been touched with a feeling of our infirmities; tempted in all points like as we are, though without sin; and then, having been "made higher than the heavens," and assumed the Throne of Universal Empire, it was further necessary that He should avail Himself of the exercise of an August Function, of which we are yet to make mention. Only on this condition could He enable Himself to succor us adequately in our temptations. (Hebrews vii. 25, 26, compared with ii. 18.) Why it was so we do not fully comprehend; it is enough that we know the fact, with its necessity and its sufficiency. The certainty, the possibility even, of our salvation to the uttermost, could have had no foundation out of the Theanthropic Reign of Christ.

But a full view has not yet been taken of the ground of necessity for this Reign. While it was required for the completion of our salvation, there were subsidiary and ulterior purposes which could not be otherwise answered. It was necessary that He should have all power in heaven and earth to carry forward His great undertaking through the coming ages of the world, and to bring the history of the world to its predestined end. Supreme authority over all nations was required. (Matt. xxviii. 18–20.) He must be the Prince of the kings and the kingdoms of the earth. (Rev. i. 5.) Rebellious empires were to be overthrown; the powers of darkness, the gates of hell were to be vanquished; Satan was to be cast out and consigned to the bottomless pit; death, the last enemy, was to be destroyed; the creature was to be delivered from the bondage of corruption; the heavens and the earth were to be renewed; the peace of the universe was to be conquered. The book of the Apocalypse gives the shadows of the things which are comprehended in the immense system of agencies and changes over which it was necessary that a government, sure of success, should be maintained. What breadths of time, what cycles of civilization, what revolutions of empire, what conflicts of kingdoms, what powers of good and evil, visible and invisible, working with and counterworking one another—even down to the end of the world! On no shoulder but that of the exalted and enthroned God-man could the government rest which the vast exigence required. Infinite Goodness, pursuing justly and wisely its end, could not dispense with the Theanthropic Kingdom.

Of this kingdom the grand distinction is that it is MEDIATORIAL or PRIESTLY. The titles God-man and Mediator are of the same significance. The monarch of this kingdom is styled "a Priest upon his Throne." (Zech. vi. 13.) The regal and sacerdotal functions are combined in His unparalleled supremacy. It is through the virtue of A SACRIFICE that He exercises the government over the world. All royal decrees, commands, distributions are fulfilled through the concurrent exercise of a great High-Priesthood—the presentation of a Sacrifice. The Sacrifice is the same that He presented when, through the Eternal Spirit, He offered Himself without spot on the Cross. The presentation now is through INTERCESSION. It implies no necessity, it does not admit of oral or formal supplications; it consists in the presence, in Heaven, of such a one as He is—the Eternal Son of God, as a Lamb which has been slain—with those scars of infinite honor in His adorable Person, which He received at His immolation. (Rev. v. 6.) These ever-glorious scars, the prints of the nails in His hands and feet, and the cleft in His side, were all conspicuous when He ascended the Throne; they have continued to be so; they constitute the INTERCESSION—the comprehensive virtue and strength of the Mediatorial Kingdom.

The duration of this kingdom is limited. It will end in the end of the world. The necessity for it will then have ceased; the purpose for which it was established will have been accomplished. The God-Man will surrender His delegated dominion to God, even the Father. (1 Cor. xv. 24.) The Mediatorial will be merged into the IMMEDIATORIAL kingdom, and the Son himself be subject to Him who put all things under Him. The Incarnate Deity will remain incarnate; in His Divinity coequal and coeternal still, as of necessity He ever must be, with the other Divine Persons; but as clothed in our nature, and as everlasting Head of His Body the Church, He will be officially subordinate to God; and thenceforth God, as such, the Eternal Three-One, be *all in all:* ALL IN ALL, in the delighted consciousness of every creature throughout the Realm of goodness and blessedness; in the exercise of government ALL IN ALL, likewise, to the apprehension and everlasting torment of unholy beings in the prison of despair.

XI.—JUSTIFICATION BY GRACE.

Man, in his first estate, being sinless or innocent, was legally just in the sight of God. Perfectly obedient to the precept of the law, he was not obnoxious to its penalty. By sinning he changed his relations to law. Might he by any means be put back into his original relations? Might he again become legally just?

Innocent again, he certainly cannot become. The same person cannot be both criminal and innocent. If he has committed an offence, he may repent of it, he may be forgiven; but the fact remains; character and condition may change, but what has been, cannot cease to have been; it may be atoned for, it cannot be abolished.

The law, then, cannot justify one who has transgressed it, if to justify means to make or pronounce innocent. The restoration of man, therefore, in respect of justification, taking this term in its strict or legal sense, is impossible. No arbitrary act of will, no imputation of another's innocence or merit, though it be the merit of *condignity*, can effect the *legal* justification of one who has broken the law. This merit can by no possibility be made his, any more than the desert of punishment can be made the desert of reward. The question whether a sinner may be justified again, in the sense in which he was justified before he transgressed the law, is, by his having transgressed it, answered in the negative.

Is it proper, then, to apply the term JUSTIFICATION to a state in relation to law, into which a sinner may by any means be brought? The fact that the term is not only so applied in Scripture, but, in this application of it, intensely emphasized and insisted upon, supersedes this question. The propriety, if not the indispensableness of using this term, in this application of it, is not a subject of legitimate inquiry or doubt. And the question, doubtless, never would have arisen —there would have been no place for it, even in thought—if just views had always been taken of the relation to law in which the Atonement puts a believer—one who avails himself of its benefit. This relation, though not that precisely which obedience to the law constitutes, is at least of equivalent virtue. It makes it unnecessary on any account to punish the believer, by answering all the ends of his punishment; and exemption from this is all that, in justice, obedience to the law can claim from God. For aught beyond this, God, in justice, can be in debt to no creature. Creatures owe God their perfect obedience; but He owes and can owe them nothing, beyond the negative good of not doing them an injury. All that He does for them, more than this, is the fruit of His goodness, not of that justice which must acknowledge and pay a debt, or become injustice. There is no creature to whom continuance in being is desirable, who is not indebted to the Divine goodness even for this. Everything, in such a creature's existence, except in so far as he may have harmed himself,—everything in so far as God's dealing with him is concerned, has been simply good, up to this moment; and if from this moment he should cease to be, there would be no abatement of that goodness of which his life, from its beginning, has been full, and no ground of complaint against God, so far as regards this creature's history. If the Power which made, and has been incessantly upholding him, should withdraw Itself, and leave him to pass back into nothness out of which it brought him, it would do him no wrong; nor might any one call It to account. God is answerable to Himself, and to Himself only, for the exercises of His Almighty power. Should He make new worlds, and, after a time, unmake them, who can say that He would not be doing right? God owes it to Himself to bless His obedient creatures; it becomes Him as the All-Perfect, the All-Good, thus to deal with them; if He has given them His promise, self-regard requires Him to fulfil it. But in respect to their personal desert or claim, its limit has been defined; they have, and can have, no merit of condignity beyond the negative one, not to be dealt with injuriously: a merit of this kind, a claim on justice, beyond that, is inconsistent with the very idea of the Deity as the Fountain of all being, and all good, and with the necessary relations between Him and His dependent creatures. (See Rom. xi. 35, 36.)

Now, so far as regards this claim, though the Atonement cannot create it, on the part of a believer, or take away from him the desert of punishment, yet it can and does take away all ground or reason for the infliction of punishment; and thus put him virtually in that relation to law, which he would have been in, if he had not broken it. It cannot be said that he would be dealt with unjustly, or as he does not deserve to be, if he should be punished; but his punishment would be unnecessary, or to no end ulterior to itself; it would be punishment for punishment's sake, which, however merited, cannot be executed where goodness bears sway. The Atonement offers itself as a substitute for punishment; as a full equivalent for it, and thus, excepting only the believer's ill-desert, as availing to form the relation to law, in respect to him, which would have existed if he had not been disobedient to it. And, as his justification, in that case, would have been simply and only a recognition of him as unamenable to punishment, that is, virtually, a justification which he obtains through the Atonement—it renders him, on the ground of a perfect equivalent or substitute for punishment, unamenable and unexposed to a penal affliction.

It may be thought that justification, in this view of it, is nothing more than pardon; but the difference is fundamental: pardon or forgiveness is included in justification (see Rom. iv. 6–8.); but pardon may be arbitrary, or, at least, for a reason, different from an atonement or a satisfaction to punitive justice. In justification there is this satisfaction, and it is precisely this which discriminates the idea of justification from that of mere mercy in whatever form. In order to constitute the justification of a sinner, there must be a pardon, but to this must be added an Atonement as its ground—a provision, the virtue of which is to put him who has the advantage of it in the same relation to the law, so far as regards the reasons for punishment, as obedience to the law constitutes and implies.

It has been thought that the term justification is not applicable to one's state in relation to law, unless this include something more than unamenableness to punishment; additional to this, he must have a *legal* title to eternal life. But this is not included even in a strictly legal justification: obedience itself confers no such title, as has been said already. A person legally justified, as long as he lives without sinning, cannot be punished: God, moreover, may owe it to Himself as good and the friend of goodness, to show such a person favor, perhaps eminent favor; but if he does, it is not a debt due to him from God in strict justice; he has no claim on his Maker, on this or any ground, even for one moment's continuance in being.

They who say that justification includes a legal title to salvation, give the Atonement the virtue of conferring this title. But if the existence of the title be an impossibility, the Atonement cannot have the virtue they ascribe to it. We have seen that a legal title, even to exemption from punishment where it has been incurred, is an impossibility. As to this, even a merit of *condignity*, a claim in law or justice, in one who has incurred it by transgression, is an absurdity, a contradiction in terms. What place, then, is there for the idea of a legal title to eternal life? And for what reason were such a title to be desired if it were a possibility? Or what advantage could it give its possessor which he may not have without it, unless it be an advantage to be free of the Divine goodness, and to have self-merit as the measure of one's happiness? A title to anything in justice, or as a debt, is not a condition of receiving good from God: He requires no such title; He is already more than willing, for the sake of the Atonement, to confer the highest favors on those to whom the only debt due from Him is eternal death. The Atonement itself was required, not from a parsimony of goodness, but rather that the way of goodness, on the largest scale, might be open and unobstructed. And the Atonement itself was the fruit of goodness, and of all its fruits unspeakably greatest. From first to last the salvation of man—the Atonement, forgiveness, eternal life, for the Atonement's sake—has goodness, not justice, not obligation, as its fountain. The whole comes, it is true, through the Atonement—the immediate producing cause of the whole. It is for Christ's sake, for the sake of His infinite sacrifice, His obedience unto death, His personal intercession, that God exalts the believer to the honors and felicities of His everlasting kingdom; treats him, to use the language of Scripture, as if he were "the righteousness of God;" justifies him with a justification which makes him a son and an heir of God, a joint-heir with Christ: But while this justification has its ground in the work of Christ, it is not on that account the less gratuitous, the less independent of a claim in justice, the less an act of pure and absolute grace. The Biblical statement of the doctrine of a sinner's justification is nowhere more complete or precise than in Romans iii. 24: "BEING JUSTIFIED FREELY BY HIS GRACE THROUGH THE REDEMPTION THAT IS IN CHRIST JESUS."

XII.—FAITH.

THERE are two senses in which the epithet *spiritual* may be applied to man: as signifying either the immaterial or spiritual part of his nature, or a certain state or quality of the latter. In the former meaning it distinguishes the soul from the body; in the other it distinguishes regenerate from unregenerate man. An unregenerate man, even in respect to his immateriality or spirit, is called carnal (1 Cor. iii. 3; Col. ii. 18); a regenerate man, as such, is called spiritual. That which is born of the Spirit is spirit; that is, has a spiritual nature like that of the Holy Spirit of whom he is born. And this new spiritual nature which comes of the second birth, has a spiritual understanding, or power of spiritual discernment (Rom. viii. 6, 7; Col. i. 9; 1 Cor. ii. 15); "A new foundation laid in the nature of the soul for a new kind of exercises of the natural understanding."* Hence the explanation of man's deliverance from that moral deceptiveness or power of infatuation in which sin begins, and by which it maintains its dominion within him. It is in the exercise of this new power or principle of nature that the spell of sin is broken, that good and evil are again discerned in their proper characters, and the reign of rectitude or goodness established.

* President Edwards.

Now that which is objectively correlative to this new principle, toward which it acts, and from which it takes its impressions, is not a direct *presentation* of things, but a *representation* of them by means of statement or testimony, namely, the Word of God—the outward witness of the Spirit. In respect to the things themselves, God is a Testifier or Affirmant, apart from whose Word there is no possibility of our knowing them, no evidence to us of their truth or existence. If they become realities to us, if they impress themselves upon us, they do so no otherwise than through the medium of this Word, which has this influence only as it is accredited or believed. This accounts for the application of the term FAITH to that use or exercise of the spiritual understanding by which we are said to discern or know these things.

It is not possible to give a strict definition of Faith. Like vision or hearing it can no otherwise be understood than by its function or what it does. In regard to this the Biblical assertion is, that Faith is what makes the contents of the Divine Word as present realities to the believer, (Heb. xi. 1). These contents—simple assertions—are matters of as perfect certitude to him as things which he sees, hears, or handles; and it is his faith which gives them this certitude. And the reason why it does this is, that that which attests them is what it is, THE WORD OF GOD. He has no conception, no knowledge of them, except what this Word gives him; they surpass his power of comprehension; many of them are futurities, which only Omniscience can know, and only Omnipotence can actualize; and were they not declared by God Himself, it would be simple credulity or folly to believe them. But because, and only because, the Mouth of God hath spoken them, they are to that new power of discernment which belongs to him as a regenerate or spiritual person, as certain and real as objects of sight are to the eye.

What gives them this reality is, the correlation between this new spiritual sense and God Himself as objective to it. It is this sense which makes the Deity in His proper nature a reality to man. The world is a revelation of the glory of God (Ps. xix. 1, Rom. i. 20); but it is such in effect only to a spiritual mind. The unregenerate are without God in the world (Eph. ii. 12). Even the inspired Word of God is no revelation to them (1 Cor. ii. 14). Being destitute of spiritual sense or understanding, there is no possibility to them of the spiritual knowledge of God any more than there is of the intellectual knowledge of Him to irrational creatures. But let one have this new sense, and God, in the glory of His nature, becomes the only reality; all being, all goodness, all else is comparatively less than nothing to Him. What then—as a ground or reason of certitude to him,—what is there in the universe superior or equal to the Word of this all-glorious Being? Is it cause for wonder, that whatever this Word contains is as obviously true and real to the soul of a believer, as the existence of the world is to his natural consciousness?

Now, among the contents of this Word, high and transcendent as the sun in the system which he illumines, is the scheme of Justification by grace. It is of course correspondently distinguished among the spiritual apprehensions of a regenerate man. His ineffable complacency in it, his joyous acceptance of it, his absolute reliance upon it, for his own personal justification, is, of course, a fact, a moral necessity. Thus it comes to pass, that he is actually justified by it; and because the event occurs through an exercise of faith, it is ascribed to Faith as its productive cause. He is said to be justified BY HIS FAITH. The connecting medium between him and the scheme of justification, is spoken of, by metonomy, as if it had in itself a justifying virtue. It is said, indeed, to be imputed to him, for righteousness; as if it were equivalent, at least, to a complete obedience of the law. The explanation has been given. It is not that faith is this in itself; it would not be this, even if it were perfect. The only substitute for obedience, or the righteousness of the law, is the Atonement—"the righteousness of God," (Rom. i. 17; iii. 21, 22); but whereas it is through the instrumentality of faith, that this righteousness becomes available to justification, so the instrument is put for its object, and is imputed or accounted as if it were this in reality.

The function of faith is not restricted to justification. From first to last, it is, on our part, the factor, the working power in our salvation. Next to the influence of the indwelling Spirit, it is the prime agent in the production of character, the perfecting of inherent righteousness in the justified. In all its acts, the first included,—that in which it justifies us,—it is a vanquisher of evil, a purifier of the heart, a former of the image of Christ within us. The same faith which appropriates justifying grace, accomplishes the whole, and does this in the self-same kind and mode of activity. It sanctifies precisely as it justifies us. In itself, an exercise of spiritual understanding or discernment terminating on its proper objects, the contents of Scripture, it gives these objects a formative influence on the soul, and moulds the character and life in conformity to them. Its efficacy is not from itself, but from the revelations of the Word of God, or more strictly from God Himself, as discerned by means of them. It is therefore, in a sense, a Divine efficacy. The Word of God gives Faith, a use as it were of the Divine attributes. It sees light in God's light, is wiser than the ancients, has an unction from the Holy One whereby it knows all things, looks into the future, sees the fulfilment of the prophecies, the second advent of Christ, the resurrection of the dead, the judgment of the world, the new heavens and earth, the end of the righteous and the wicked: The whole is reality to Faith. Moreover, it can do all things, remove mountains, quench the violence of fire, subdue kingdoms, overcome the world. It can command whatever it will; ask and receive what it will; fill itself with all the fulness of God: Nothing is impossible to it: So it is written in the Word of God— that Word which to Faith is as God Himself. Of course, it is to be taken in a consistency with whatever else that Word contains: for its contents are a unit, each cognate and co-organized with every other and with the whole; but it is not hereby deprived of its own proper significance, a significance not diminished but increased in value by its organic relations, and not to be misapprehended by Faith.

Three conclusions follow: In the first place, that the first concern of a believer, is to have his faith always in lively and vigorous exercise. Only let him *believe*. In proportion to the measure of his faith will be the measure of his attainment in personal virtue or conformity to Christ; the measure of his good works or usefulness in the world; the measure of his meetness for the blessedness of heaven. And, that he may be mature and strong in faith, it is necessary, in the next place, that he keep the principle of faith, the spiritual sense of which faith is an exercise in its normal condition; in order to do which, thirdly, the chief prerequisite is, that he grieve not the indwelling Spirit of God, the author and vitalizer of this principle and of all its activity. This last practically includes the others; they will not, cannot be wanting, when the Spirit is not grieved; and therefore this precept, "grieve not, quench not the Spirit," may be propounded as the summary or compend of all his concern.

XIII.—CHARACTER OF BELIEVERS.

The chief excellence of the good is in themselves, not in their works; in their character, not in their manifestations of it. However high their estimation in respect of the latter, it is as nothing compared with that of their inherent excellence. The revealed glory of the Deity, which fills the world with its effulgence, is but a faint ray of the immanent perfection of His Nature. But there is a distinction, a higher and a lower, in inherent excellence itself. The spiritual is superior to the natural, the moral to the constitutional. The latter, indeed, is but in order to the former, from its subordinate relation to which it takes its highest value. It is the chief glory of the Divine attributes, that they are all, if we may so speak, in the service of Love, the essence and sum of moral rectitude or goodness.

In the ground of our justification by grace, there is no place for any righteousness or moral excellence of ours; and there is no necessity for it. The Atonement is all sufficient for its purpose, without addition from us. It were, moreover, offering the highest affront to infinite excellence; it were arrogating a justifying virtue to that which needs to be justified; it were bringing guilt to assist in justifying the guilty; it were seeking to combine pollution with a purity, in the presence of which " the heavens are not clean," to attempt making an addition to it: An iniquity too common among men, and not less perilous and hurtful than common.

But it is not to be hence concluded, that personal righteousness or moral excellence, on our part, may be dispensed with in our justification, or that we may be justified by grace, while still unjust in ourselves, or disobedient to the law. Justification allows no inversion of the scale of excellence ; no place for the idea that character is less valuable than condition, or that personal goodness is unessential to the favor of God. Justification, on the contrary, is itself in order to a good character ; of which, the germ is already in us when it takes place, and the full maturity and perfection already provided for and secured. In the act of justifying us, God begins the fulfilment of a scheme of agency, each part of which is interconnected with the whole, and with every other part. In its time and order, the presence of no part can be wanting. The scheme is a unit. The first part anticipates the last. Whom He justifies, them He sanctifies, and, in due time, He also glorifies.

While, therefore, justification and personal virtue are distinct, they are inseparable from each other. The former, a single act, is already complete ; the latter, a gradual formation, is also sure of eventual completion. Simultaneously with the moment of justification, the Holy Spirit begins His appropriate function within us. It is through this beginning that we meet the indispensable condition of our justification.

Having already entered our perverted nature, the Spirit regenerates it, renews it, assimilates it to His own; and thus delivering it from the dominion of sin, giving truth and falsehood, good and evil, their just appearances again, making old things to pass away and all things to become new to us, He evokes our complacency in the glorious plan of justification by grace, as set before us in the inspired Word, so that we joyfully adopt and accept it as our own. Nor does He rest here. He has come into us, as into His temple, His everlasting habitation, out of which He is never more to depart. Henceforth the supreme dominion within us is that of rectitude. Our reason, our conscience, our intelligence, our affections, our acts of willing, our spirit, our habits and ways of life, are inviolably consecrated to personal virtue. Such is the security for good character in the justified. It is as sufficient for its purpose, as the Atonement is for our justification before God.

For substance, personal righteousness, or moral excellence, is universally the same; the same in heaven and on earth, in God and the angels, in man before his fall and after his restoration. But like intelligence and physical life, it is modified by its surroundings, the external agencies which exert themselves upon it. In respect to justified man, these are wondrously distinctive and peculiar. The mode of his justification, as an objective power, has an influence upon him to which there is no parallel, and which is necessarily foreign and strange to others. In the reversal of his doom to eternal death; in the obliteration of his countless impurities and offences; in the immeasurable, all-amazing contrast between what he was, and what he has become; and above all, in the Great Propitiation through which he is justified, there are motives, elements of purity, of which he alone can be conscious, and such as cannot but give him a transcendent peculiarity of personal character.

But there is yet another demand for peculiarity. The plan of justifying grace comprehends our conformity to an unparalleled pattern or type of personal virtue; even of that self-same type, by the exercise of which the Atonement was made, the way for our justification by grace prepared. After the very example of that righteousness through the virtue of which we are justified, we ourselves are required to become righteous. The character of Christ is to be produced in us. That very stamp or distinction of righteousness which he displayed in His humiliation and death on our behalf, we ourselves are to bear. The same mind is to be in us which was also in Him when, being in the Form of God and equal with God, He emptied Himself, and took upon Him the Form of a servant, and was made in the likeness of man; and being found in fashion as a man, humbled Himself, and became obedient unto death, even the death of the Cross (Phil. ii. 5–8). In making the Atonement Christ was alone; no creature could take part with Him in that. But in the spirit in which He performed that work, the character so strange and peculiar which He displayed in performing it, we are to be like Him, precisely and perfectly like Him—conformed to Him without exception or reserve. This conformity on our part—elemental at first, and at last complete—is the true exponent or significance of the condition of our being justified by His atoning death; and this not by an arbitrary arrangement, but by the requisition of essential rectitude. We should be without the principle of personal virtue if we should be found wanting in this conformity; if the same love in kind, wherewith He loved us when He died for our sins had no place in our hearts; nay, if it did not actually reproduce His character in us. When the Apostle speaks of his being crucified with Christ, of his being made conformable to the death of Christ, of his bearing about in his body the dying of the Lord Jesus, that the life also of Jesus might be manifest in his body, he does but give himself as a specimen of the character which is proper and requisite in all who are justified by grace. This mode of justification demands such a character, and virtue itself is disowned where the demand is not met.

On no point is Biblical teaching more full and impressive than on this—the essential identity in character between Christ and ourselves. Recur to our Lord's frequent discourses on it to His disciples: recur especially to the prayer which He offered on their behalf before His Passion, the great burden of which was this very thing: call to mind the declaration that God has predestinated us to be conformed to the image of His Son: study the meaning of the Scripture where it calls us the brethren of Christ, and Him the First-born among many brethren, and makes us members of His body, of His flesh, and of His bones, and identifies us with Him, in His death, His burial, His resurrection, His ascension, and His glory in Heaven: Mark attentively the Biblical representation of the Spirit's method of working in sanctifying us: how He ever keeps the image of Christ before us; takes of the things of Christ and shows them to us; changes us into His likeness more and more, from glory to glory; forms Him within us the hope of glory, and ceases not until our resemblance to Him is perfect and entire, wanting nothing. It is not simply virtue or righteousness that is needed, but that mode or fashion of it of which the only example, in this or any world, is that of the God-man our Saviour.

Such then is that peculiarity of character or inherent righteousness, which belongs to those who are justified by grace. It is individual and unique. It has no parallel, no similitude, among men or angels. As to their subjective virtue, angels are not altogether what they were before they knew the depth to which the Divine Goodness could descend in the form of mercy to man. The manifestations of this mercy cannot but modify and immeasurably enhance the virtue and consequently the happiness of the universe. But justified man must have forever an individuality of character of which no other can partake. Others will be one with him in celebrating the praise of justifying mercy (Rev. v. 11, 12); but there is one act of worship in which they cannot take part: they cannot sing with the justified, "Unto Him that loved us and washed us from our sins in His blood;" and the subjective difference which hinders them from uniting in this song has, as to its ground, a breadth and a length, a depth and height, which passes finite knowledge.

Among men, all but the justified are entire strangers to virtue. There is to them no alternative, but either to be virtuous with that peerless virtue which is the companion and fruit of justifying grace, or to be destitute of the germ and life of virtue. It is common to commend the pursuit of virtue, without reference to this grace as prerequisite to it—sometimes as preparatory to our receiving it; sometimes not only as possible but sufficient without it; sometimes with contempt for it as antagonistic to virtue: But if an effect cannot be without its cause, if we cannot have sunbeams apart from the sun, neither can man be virtuous or inherently just, without being already just with God, through justification by grace. The first concern of man is to accept the Atonement; to reject it, is to love a twofold death—death under the condemnatory sentence of immutable law and rectitude, and death as to the hope of restoration to rectitude or virtue. It is sin refusing to be forgiven, guilt too proud to accept of justifying grace; it is also the foul and bitter waters of inborn corruption, refusing to be displaced by a well of celestial water springing up into the life of everlasting purity and joy. After it may remain, what doubtless were before it, activities of conscience and natural affection, struggles to be just with God; good works, so called, but no virtue, and no sufficiency for virtue; nay, it necessitates an invigoration of the principle of sin, and a new guilt greater than the first.

As to appropriate character in the justified, it has been already said that its formation is gradual. Its beginning, like that of our natural existence, is rudimental or embryonic; its development is often retarded, sometimes even regressive; it has to endure manifold contentions from within and from without; it is sometimes overborne in its conflicts, and for a season seems to be extinct: but it eventually prevails, over its adversaries,—through all its changes progresses to completion, and at length appears pure amid the purities of Heaven, a perfect resemblance to the character of Christ.

XIV.—TRUTH THE SAME AND ALWAYS YOUNG:
THE OLD IN THE NEW.

"I write no new commandment unto you, but the old commandment which ye had from the beginning. Again, a new commandment I write unto you."* It is common in popular discourse, to contradict our own assertions immediately after making them—to say what we go on to deny, or deny what we have just said; we are not, however, in such cases, inconsistent with ourselves, nor do we speak inadvertently; our design is to set the thing we speak of into contrast with itself, under different aspects. We speak of the thing in the second instance, in a different relation, or with a different reference from that which we intended in the first. The apostle does not contradict himself, when, after saying, " I write no new commandment," he adds, in the following sentence, "Again, a new commandment I write." What he wrote was, for substance, " the word which the church had had from the beginning." It was, therefore, nothing new. But yet it was new in a sense, on account of the new light which was shining in respect to it; the new associations and enforcements it had received — the fullness of meaning which it had been shown to contain.

* 1 John ii. 7, 8.

There has been but one true religion. There are two Testaments; but the religion they contain is one. Christianity, the new commandment of the apostle, is but the faith of the antediluvian elders in its maturity and completeness. The books of the New Testament, in their historical, doctrinal, and ethical details, and in their diversified style, diction, examples, illustrations, are but the perfect edition of a religion, the rudiments of which were given to man by his Maker near the beginning of his existence; regarding it in its date, it was old; regarding it in the stage of development which it had reached, it was strangely new: eye had not seen, ear had not heard it; the thought of it had not entered into the heart of man.

The apostle might speak of it as new, comparing it with itself under the latest of its antecedent forms; those not only of the last of the prophets, and of the harbinger of our Lord, but of our Lord Himself, previous to His ascension. Even during his personal ministry, there was scarcely the twilight of evangelical truth, when compared with the full-day brightness with which it shone after the baptism of the Holy Ghost and of fire.

Nor have the epithets old and new ceased to be applicable to Christianity. There has been progress in the knowledge of Christianity—progress from vagueness to precision, from obscurity to splendor, in some points—since the days of the apostles. There have been no authentic additions to it; but new representations and impressions have been given of it, from time to time, in virtue of which it has been itself called new. At different epochs, it has become almost as new as it was at first, in its new manifestations of power, and in the new impressions which men have had of it. It was so in the early part of the sixteenth century, when its republication by the reformers, was as a resurrection of it to the nations of Europe. Indeed, at every period of awakening in the church, the ancient faith becomes new again. Nay, it is, as it were, constantly rejuvenizing itself in the experience of individual Christians, to many of whom it seems to be always becoming more and more novel. The old, primitive word, the same essentially, yesterday, to-day and forever, appears to them each day more fresh than when it first opened itself to them. It is always recognized by them as the same old commandment, but it has a new aspect; everything in it looks perfectly fresh and young; its facts, teachings, tendencies, bearings, relations, influences, are ever and more and more new.

This power of self-rejuvenescence, this old-new, or new-old life of our religion, is what makes it a religion for all time—for universal man, till the end of the world. It would not otherwise have a permanently saving power. It does not possess this power, as being simply historic, that is to say, not a myth or fabulous, but founded in fact; this is necessary, but not sufficient: to meet the wants of man in successive generations, Christianity must be unlike other religions in two respects—not only in having a ground, as they have not, in veritable history, but also in having power to renovate and reproduce its ground, so as to make it no less real and manifest to others of the remotest times, than it was to those who lived in the beginning. The past must return in the present; antiquity must reappear in novelty: a merely historic religion is not an available one—does not, cannot answer the purpose of religion. Dying man needs a Saviour, and one inhabiting the present equally with the past, and one, moreover, present to him, and with him, as he walks through the valley of the shadow of death, more really, more perfectly, than any fellow-mortal can be at any time. The ability of the Christian history, of the ground-fact of Christianity, to reproduce itself in the present, to be always fresh, young, palpable, as at first, in the experience of believers, is, in truth, its saving ability. Christianity, divine in its essence—a divine life, as well as a divine doctrine—having its spring in God—and being vitalized and sustained by the indwelling Spirit of God—being, moreover, not only historic, but the key of history—its Author being the Creator and Ruler of the world, who orders the events of time with reference to its advancement, and to the same end exerts, when He pleases, supernatural forces: Hence its permanent efficiency as a religion for man; its antiquity and also its perpetual and progressive novelty, its venerable age, and also its eternal youth and freshness.

This two-fold characteristic of Christianity has given rise to a principle of classification and division in the church. The epithets *old* and *new*, from this, as the occasion, have been applied to different classes of Christians. Among Christians, as among men, some are constitutionally conservative, some versatile and impulsive: hence antagonisms, "sides," "schools," "lights"—one called *old* from their attachment to the oldness, the antiquity of Christianity; the other *new*, from their characteristic susceptibility to the power of the novelty in which Christianity arrays itself from time to time.

This susceptibility implies no comparison of old and new in Christianity itself, no ground or possibility of a difference between Christianity at first and afterwards, but only a special liveliness or impressibility to new manifestations of what is, in itself, old. It implies no want of interest or delight in the old faith— it is, in truth, this delight, this interest itself. The novelty, whose power is felt, is not absolute novelty; it is antiquity in novelty; the new does but reproduce the old; it is the same old Christianity which the apostles preached, giving new proofs of its identity, and of its invincible, undying, ever-efficient power to save. It is not a reproach, it is not weakness, to be perfectly alive to novelty, under this idea of it. It is honorable to be called new for such a reason, and more so than old, if the latter term is to be understood in a sense implying that the other is not honorable.

This *nominal* distinctiveness has no necessary connection with sectarianism: that is the bane of Christianity, but this, apart from the spirit of sect, is but diversity in unity, which in the scheme of the world and in Deity itself, is the condition of perfection. *In veste Christi varietas sit, non scissura sit.*

www.ingramcontent.com/pod-product-compliance
Lightning Source LLC
Chambersburg PA
CBHW031329230426
43670CB00006B/284